THE FOUR PATHS OF ASSERTIVENESS

the four paths of assertiveness

Speaking Up,
Jumping In,
Embracing Compassion,
and Accepting Life

Scott Cooper and
Naoki Yoshinaga, PhD

Johns Hopkins University Press
Baltimore

© 2025 Scott Cooper and Naoki Yoshinaga
All rights reserved. Published 2025
Printed in the United States of America on acid-free paper
9 8 7 6 5 4 3 2 1

Johns Hopkins University Press
2715 North Charles Street
Baltimore, Maryland 21218
www.press.jhu.edu

Library of Congress Cataloging-in-Publication Data

Names: Cooper, Scott, author. | Yoshinaga, Naoki, author.
Title: The four paths of assertiveness : speaking up, jumping in, embracing compassion, and accepting life / Scott Cooper and Naoki Yoshinaga, PhD.
Description: Baltimore : Johns Hopkins University Press, 2024. | Includes bibliographical references and index.
Identifiers: LCCN 2024025709 | ISBN 9781421451176 (hardcover) | ISBN 9781421451183 (paperback) | ISBN 9781421451190 (epub)
Subjects: LCSH: Assertiveness (Psychology) | Interpersonal relations.
Classification: LCC BF575.A85 C67 2024 | DDC 158.2—dc23/eng/20240724
LC record available at https://lccn.loc.gov/2024025709

A catalog record for this book is available from the British Library.

Special discounts are available for bulk purchases of this book.
For more information, please contact Special Sales at specialsales@jh.edu.

To Julie

To Mikiko

CONTENTS

Acknowledgments *ix*

Introduction
A Broader View of Assertiveness *1*

1. Speaking Up
Social Assertiveness *13*

2. Jumping In
Behavioral Assertiveness *56*

3. Embracing Compassion
Emotional Assertiveness *77*

4. Accepting Life
Mental Assertiveness *96*

Afterword
Happiness Research and These Four Paths *124*

Notes *139*
Selected Bibliography *153*
Index *157*

ACKNOWLEDGMENTS

FROM SCOTT COOPER

Many thanks to Johns Hopkins University Press for publishing our book, with a special thank-you to our editor Suzanne Staszak-Silva and her colleagues for their excellent guidance and leadership; this includes our very adept copyeditor Kathleen Capels and production editor Robert Brown. Thank-you to Eric Braun for his valued early editorial input and to Becky Cabaza for her kind and wise advice along the way. Also special thanks to Betsy Rapoport, former Random House editor, who several years ago made the decision that first provided me with the opportunity to write on the important topic of assertiveness for young people. A grateful thank-you to my parents, who exemplified kindness and independence of thought. Also to my brother, Jed Cooper, for his helpful insights for the last section of chapter four. As usual, a very big thank-you to Julie for her extremely valuable review and input. I'm very lucky to have her in my life. Last, but not least, thank-you to my coauthor, Naoki Yoshinaga. He has a very full and accomplished academic and professional career, and I greatly appreciate his carving out the time to share his wisdom and experience. It's been a privilege to work with him on this book.

FROM NAOKI YOSHINAGA

I am grateful to Johns Hopkins University Press for its support and belief in this project. Special thanks are owed to Suzanne Staszak-Silva and her colleagues for their meticulous editorial work, which greatly enhanced the clarity and coherence of this manuscript. I extend my heartfelt appreciation to Scott Cooper, whose original conceptualization of this book laid the foundation on which it stands. His guidance and expertise have been instrumental in shaping its development, and I am fortunate to have benefited from his knowledge and experience. I would also like to express my deepest gratitude to my wife, Mikiko, whose unwavering support and encouragement have been a source of strength throughout this journey.

Introduction

A Broader View of Assertiveness

This book is about traditional assertiveness: helping you deal with difficult people, stand up for yourself, and advocate for what's right. It's about learning to become more skillful at speaking up. We humans don't enjoy being rolled over by others, whether those others are employers, coworkers, customers, family, friends, neighbors, or larger social, political, and commercial forces. We believe this book contains the best tools available for helping you respond to difficult social interactions.

But full assertiveness is about much more. It's about taking greater charge of your life. Our well-being not only is impacted by our interactions with others (our social worlds), but it's also affected by what we do (our behavioral worlds), what we feel (our emotional worlds), and what we think (our mental worlds). Taking charge of our lives means assertively taking action in each of these four key areas of living. In addition to traditional assertiveness tools, this book will give you practical tools geared to a larger definition of assertiveness: *taking intentional actions that foster our social, behavioral, emotional, and mental well-being. And those actions are defined as **speaking up, jumping in, embracing compassion, and accepting life**.* We take the position that behavioral activation, compassion, and acceptance are just as importantly assertive as speaking up.

IF NOT NOW, WHEN?

It's clear in our contemporary world that adults want to take greater charge of their lives. The "great resignation" that occurred during the recent global pandemic is a powerful example. This social phenomenon, where employees left their jobs en masse in early 2021, was fueled by people assertively determining where and how they wanted to live out their lives—right now.[1] An additional example is Millennials' strong desire to make a difference by taking social stands and advancing a cause. Whether the issue involves gender and racial equality and fairness or environmental responsibility, this generation of adults is motivated to initiate tangible, positive change. But we also see more immediate evidence of this desire for having a greater degree of self-determination in the midst of the mundane comings and goings of our everyday lives. Each of us wants to engage more fully in those activities and relationships that bring us joy and satisfaction and invest less in the ones that do not. We don't want to simply stand by and watch our lives get swallowed up by things we don't value. We are asking, with ever greater sincerity and urgency, If not now, when?

This book provides specific tools to help you, as readers, in this endeavor to take greater intentional ownership of your lives both externally (socially and behaviorally) and internally (emotionally and mentally). This is not always instinctive or easy to do, but learning about specific tools coming out of happiness studies and modern psychology can help.

WHY THESE FOUR PATHS

The four paths of assertiveness featured in this book are focused on proven principles of intentional behavior that foster well-being. They are grounded in several decades of happiness studies (briefly discussed in the afterword) that define happiness (i.e., subjective well-being) as composed of two critical factors: (1) life satisfaction, and (2) positive emotions. We believe that assertiveness for its own sake isn't very helpful if it doesn't foster subjective well-being.

Fifty percent or more of our happiness is likely based on the genetic predispositions we're born with (our happiness set point). Life circumstances—such as income, health, age, and marital status—don't have the impact on well-being that we might expect, because we tend to adapt to our changing life circumstances (both good and bad) and revert to the level of our happiness set point. As noted in the afterword, life circumstances may account for only about 10 percent of our happiness.[2] This leaves *intentional activities* (what we assertively choose to do and think) as the lever we can use to make a difference in our well-being. Despite our genetic predispositions and life circumstances, we can impact our well-being through the intentional behaviors that we pursue. And we believe that four of the most important such behaviors are *speaking up*, *jumping in*, *embracing compassion*, and *accepting life*. Our view is that if these are the only intentional, assertive strategies that you take on in your social, behavioral, emotional, and mental worlds, your well-being in each of those domains of living will benefit greatly.

- **Speaking up** (social assertiveness) can significantly impact our happiness by fostering self-determination and fair treatment, and by helping us maintain healthy and respectful relationships with others. We define social assertiveness as *directly expressing what we want and how we feel, without the intent of rolling over other people.*

- **Jumping in** (behavioral assertiveness) is essential in obtaining what we want out of life. Life satisfaction is simply not possible without jumping in. It has repeatedly been demonstrated that jumping into enjoyable and meaningful activities can be valuable in reducing anxiety and depression. We define behavioral assertiveness as *initiating needful or desired intentional activities, even when we don't feel like it.*

- **Embracing compassion** (emotional assertiveness) is critical for responding to the biggest emotional challenge of to our well-being—suffering. Compassion benefits not only the receiver, but also the giver. We define emotional assertiveness as *intentionally responding to suffering through helpful words and actions.*

- **Accepting life** (mental assertiveness) is a key aspect in coping with the ups and downs of everyday living. Our natural instinct to make judgments can be a prime source of daily dissatisfaction and negative emotions, and the softening impact of acceptance can be a major contributor to happiness. We define mental assertiveness as *intentionally reducing unneeded negative judgment.*

Each chapter in this book focuses on one of these skill sets and discusses the challenges they help us address in our multifaceted world. Table I.1 summarizes these four paths of assertiveness, along with the rationale for their inclusion and their impact on happiness.

A TOOL KIT OF IDEAS

For a relatively small book, *The Four Paths of Assertiveness* contains a lot of information. Yet each of the principles incorporated as part of this broadened definition of assertiveness is critical. Because of its abundance of information, think of this book not as a prescriptive road map, but as a tool kit of practical ideas, and select those tools that apply to you. If you feel as though you already have enough life satisfaction and sufficient positive emotions, then you probably will have less need for a book like this. Our own view, however, is that—in the same way as we need to learn how to read, swim, or do math—most of us need to learn at least a few social and personal assertiveness skills to enhance our life satisfaction and soften unhelpful negative emotions. The purpose of this book is to provide some of these skill sets in a form that we hope makes them clear and usable. Each chapter provides discrete phrases you can use or actions you can take in specific situations. Practice relevant skills and employ them as needed.

Even if you don't remember the details and the applicable tools for each principle, we believe that anyone will not go too far astray in fostering well-being by simply remembering and returning to the spirit of these four basic paths of assertiveness, particularly in times of difficulties and unhappiness: speaking up, jumping in, embracing compassion, and accepting life. Our stay on this planet is relatively brief, so it's never too late to assert ourselves in authentic and meaningful ways that nurture well-being for ourselves and others.

Table I.1 Four paths of assertiveness, with references to research

Path of assertiveness	Impact on life satisfaction	Impact on positive and negative emotions
With **speaking up**, we assert ourselves by saying what we want and how feel, even when our natural instinct might be to fight with or flee from others.	Life satisfaction means obtaining what we realistically need. This, in turn, requires direct, honest, and respectful communication.	Numerous studies confirm that social assertiveness training is helpful in reducing symptoms of socially generated anxiety and depression, as well as in improving relationships and measures of self-esteem.[1]
With **jumping in**, we assert ourselves by initiating things we need or want to do, even when we don't feel like it.	Life satisfaction is defined as the degree to which we have what we want out of life. Life satisfaction is not possible without activating behaviors.	Several randomized controlled trials and meta-analyses provide evidence that behavioral activation (jumping into an activity) is as effective in dealing with depression as cognitive behavioral techniques and certain antidepressant drugs.[2]
With **embracing compassion**, we assert ourselves in responding to the suffering of others or ourselves, even when our natural instinct might be a lack of concern.	A major longitudinal study in Germany confirms that goals and activities involving altruism can result in significant long-term increases in life satisfaction.[3] A growing body of research demonstrates that helping others is often associated with positive mental health outcomes for the helper.[4]	Compassion itself can be a positive emotion and is connected to two other positive emotions: kindheartedness and sympathy. Research has demonstrated that people experience more positive emotions when spending money on others, rather than spending it on themselves.[5]
With **accepting life**, we assert ourselves by taking things into perspective and softening judgments when confronted with the ups and downs of life, even when our natural instinct is to have negative judgments.	By accepting the realities of life with fewer negative judgments, our satisfaction with life increases.	Acceptance is the foundation for contentment and love, two of the most beneficial positive emotions. Several researchers have found that greater acceptance can accompany less anxiety and depression. Acceptance entails softening negative judgments, which, in turn, can directly reduce negative emotions.[6]

1 Brittany C. Speed, Brandon L. Goldstein, and Marvin R. Goldfried, "Assertiveness training: A forgotten evidence-based treatment," *Clinical Psychology: Science and Practice* 25, no. 1 (March 2018): article e12216, https://doi.org/10.1111/cpsp.12216.

2 Sona Dimidjian et al., "Randomized trial of behavioral activation, cognitive therapy, and antidepressant medication in the acute treatment of adults with major depression," *Journal of Consulting and Clinical Psychology* 74, no. 4 (August 2006): 658–670, https://doi.org/10.1037/0022-006X.74.4.658; Trevor Mazzucchelli, Robert Kane, and Clare Rees, "Behavioral activation treatments for depression in adults: A meta-analysis and review," *Clinical Psychology: Science and Practice* 16, no. 4 (December 2009): 383–411, https://doi.org/10.1111/j.1468-2850.2009.01178.x.

3 Bruce Headey, Ruud Muffels, and Gert G. Wagner, "Long-running German panel survey shows that personal and economic choices, not just genes, matter for happiness," *PNAS* [*Proceedings of the National Academy of Sciences*] 107, no. 42 (October 2010): 17922–17926, https://doi.org/10.1073/pnas.1008612107.

4 For a review, see Stephanie L. Brown and R. Michael Brown, "Connecting prosocial behavior to improved physical health: Contributions from the neurobiology of parenting," *Neuroscience & Biobehavioral Reviews* 55 (August 2015): 1–17, https://doi.org/10.1016/j.neubiorev.2015.04.004.

5 Elizabeth W. Dunn, Lara B. Aknin, and Michael I. Norton, "Prosocial spending and happiness: Using money to benefit others pays off," *Current Directions in Psychological Science* 23, no. 1 (February 2014): 41–47, https://doi.org/10.1177/0963721413512503.

6 John C. Williams and Steven Jay Lynn, "Acceptance: An historical and conceptual review," *Imagination, Cognition and Personality* 30, no. 1 (September 2010): 5–56, https://doi.org/10.2190/IC.30.1.c.

INTRODUCTORY COMMENTS FROM SCOTT COOPER

The first two books I read on assertiveness were *When I Say No, I Feel Guilty*, by Manuel Smith, and *Pulling Your Own Strings*, by Wayne Dyer. These types of books had been around for a while, but they held no interest for me. Things changed, however. I was an older sophomore in college, recently married, and teaching on a part-time basis, thus feeling the stress of interacting with a lot of people. One of my bosses presented a particular challenge. He could be manipulative, unreasonable when arranging my schedule, and condescending. Looking back, I'm pretty sure I was working for a prototype of Michael Scott in the sitcom *The Office*. I mostly just smiled, said yes, and put up with it all.

But my boss wasn't completely to blame. He was who he was, and I just didn't know how to deal with him. As I looked around, I began to see a clear pattern. Whether I was dealing with an unfriendly staff member, a stern professor, an unhelpful mechanic, or almost anyone with whom I was trying to resolve a problem, too often I ended up holding a smiley, polite bag of nothing as my fellow humans abruptly moved on.

So I now had real interest in the kinds of books I previously thought had been unworthy of my attention. Some of the ideas coming out of Manuel Smith's book, in particular, provided simple verbal tools for dealing with people more directly and honestly, including feeling more comfortable with telling them no. It provided tools for dealing with conflicts without a flight-or-fight attitude. Moreover, these tools were based not just on theory, but also on his years of pioneering work in assertiveness training with Peace Corps volunteers, veterans, and many others. I quickly came to realize the value of learning specific skills to deal with difficult social situations. Despite the fact that none of this was emotionally easy at first, it was all quite liberating. I still felt some guilt in saying no, and I still felt dumb asking certain questions. I still didn't like confrontations. But I discovered that you can still say the words, even if you feel uneasy or nervous. But you do need to say the words, and you've got to be persistent.

The students I was teaching weren't much younger than I was, and I began to pass along some of these simple tools. They began speaking more directly and honestly with each other and with me, asking simple questions and resolving conflicts with less combativeness or avoidance and more of a focus on problem solving. I discovered that the power of assertive communication is not only that it helps people navigate difficult interactions, but it also promotes more direct, honest, positive, and respectful communication in general. This is something that benefits us in all types of situations.

Thus began my lifelong interest in assertiveness. Over time, I conducted more in-depth research on the topic. In 2000, I wrote my first book on assertive social skills for young people, *Sticks and Stones*. My widely distributed *Speak Up and Get Along!* was published in 2004 (with a second edition in 2019). These books have given me a platform for advocacy in the United States in the area of social assertiveness skills for young people, including bullying prevention and online safety. I continue to strongly believe that teaching young people to communicate directly, honestly, and respectfully remains a fundamentally critical endeavor. Speaking up is the first step in stopping all forms of cruelty and abuse. It's also the first step in countering the heart-breaking trend of increased suicide among young people. Individuals of all ages need to be taught to feel comfortable speaking up when undergoing extreme physical and emotional pain.

In writing these books and doing the research for them, it became overwhelmingly clear that asserting ourselves in support of our own well-being, as well as in that of others, goes beyond speaking up. In addition to our social worlds, we intimately experience our behavioral, emotional, and mental worlds. We need skills to help us assertively deal with the behaviors, unpleasant emotions, and thoughts that can make both our personal and social lives more difficult and less happy. In my books for young people, I included some of these additional personal assertiveness skills—skills coming out of cognitive behavioral psychology and acceptance-mindfulness practice. There are a variety of intentional tools that come out of these two realms, and studies throughout the years have confirmed their value. In my estimation, none are more important than the four assertive skill sets that are the focus of this book.

Assertiveness, of course, is just as important for adults as it is for young people. The young people I originally wrote my books for are now young adults, and I believe that adult assertiveness for them—and for all of us—is more valuable than ever. As my coauthor and I surveyed current publications on assertiveness for adults, we concluded that a new book on assertiveness, with an expanded definition and specific tools, was very much needed.

INTRODUCTORY COMMENTS FROM NAOKI YOSHINAGA

I come to this book as a researcher and university professor in Japan. I'm also a practicing licensed psychologist. As a cognitive behavioral therapist, both my professional work and my passion are focused on helping others take on intentional beliefs and behaviors that will make their lives happier and more effective.

I have conducted research in the areas of assertiveness and behavioral activation, and I've also been actively teaching assertiveness skills to undergraduate nursing students and working hospital nurses. Surveys tell us that, across the globe, nurses can sometimes behave passively, conforming to the stereotype of a "nice nurse," and are less likely to disagree with others in the workplace. A lower level of assertiveness in nurses is related to increased interpersonal stress, less commitment to their work, burnout, and a greater intention to leave the profession.[3] This is not a trivial problem. The world will face an acute shortage of nurses by 2030—4.8 million—according to a report from the World Health Organization.[4] I believe that assertiveness is one of the most important life skills for nurses to develop in order to reduce interpersonal stress, build effective team collaboration, prevent medical errors, and provide effective nursing care. This is supported by numerous scientific studies that have highlighted the various beneficial effects of enhancing communication through assertiveness-training programs.

And what is true for nurses is true for many of us, regardless of our chosen profession. The challenge is that most standard assertiveness-training programs require over 10 hours to complete. Since only a limited number of people have the opportunity or the motivation to receive intense assertiveness training, a self-study approach is urgently needed. I believe this book provides an opportunity for many more people to acquire the knowledge, skills, and perspectives necessary to improve their personal assertiveness.

Part of my work as a researcher and practitioner has been in investigating and providing cognitive behavioral therapy

(CBT) to help people who suffer from social anxiety. I'm currently working with researchers at the University of Oxford to develop and evaluate a culturally adapted, internet-based therapy program. Studies, as well as my international research and clinical experience to date, have shown that—regardless of cultural background, ethnicity, or gender—higher social anxiety is associated with lower assertiveness behavior to some degree.

Yet having the tools for speaking up (i.e., traditional assertiveness) is not enough. There are other important elements of assertiveness, which might not be typically thought of as assertiveness per se. A modified training program I developed for nurses has incorporated additional CBT techniques that help nurses modify their fear of negative evaluations by others before entering social situations and initiating social interactions, even when they feel uneasy. It's my belief that assertiveness is enhanced not just by speaking up, but also by activating desired behaviors (even when we're afraid) and taking on more realistic and healthy beliefs about oneself and others (with greater compassion and acceptance). This broader definition of assertiveness is the basis for this book.

Last, but not least, I want to introduce a key principle of CBT that relates to social anxiety and to developing a greater degree of assertiveness—therapy is not trying to change you, but rather is giving the real you a chance to appear more often. I believe this book can make it happen. By living our lives more intentionally (i.e., more assertively) our authentic selves are able to blossom more fully, resulting in greater life satisfaction. I believe that the simple (but comprehensive), practical, and essential four paths of assertiveness presented in this book will help people blossom.

CHAPTER 1

Speaking Up

Social Assertiveness

We define social assertiveness as *directly expressing what we want and how we feel, without the intent of rolling over other people*. We believe that this simple skill, in all its variations, is one of the most powerful skills you will ever learn to enhance your social well-being.

Our natural emotional reaction to difficult social situations can quite often lead to fight-or-flight reflexes. When we perceive a threat, we feel anger or fear, and we might automatically lash out or seek to escape. Verbal assertiveness is an effective third option—not driven by our emotions, but by mental intent. By consciously engaging in direct communication, we can let go of fight-or-flight responses (even if we still feel them) and instead use verbal and problem-solving skills. Through the application of such skills, we can maintain our own self-determination, while also developing healthy and respectful relationships with others. This, in turn, fosters greater life satisfaction.

- Instead of being intimidated or manipulated by bosses or coworkers, we can directly and more comfortably protect our own interests and self-respect.
- Instead of being a victim of ridicule and meanness from rude and difficult people in our everyday lives, we can

more artfully respond by turning attention back on them.

- Instead of dealing with conflict by fighting or avoiding problems (thus letting them fester and grow), we can use verbal and problem-solving skills to create solutions.
- In our dealings with those we love, we can simply and respectfully express ourselves without throwing in the guilt-inducing and manipulative language that we may be in the habit of using—and thus avoid the negative impact such language can have on key relationships.
- If we see social or environmental problems or other causes that are important to us, we can speak up directly and clearly, rather than remaining on the sidelines.

Assertiveness doesn't mean aggression. Aggression (i.e., forceful, unfriendly confrontation) can be the right response in extreme cases, such as protecting ourselves and others from cruelty, abuse, or danger. Instinctual anger helps us quickly prepare our bodies for self-protection, just as instinctual fear prepares our bodies for urgent escape. There are moments when our fight-or-flight instincts are crucial for our physical survival. There are many social instances, however, when a desire to fight or flee do not serve us well. Fighting often makes things worse and can hurt relationships. Fleeing allows issues to fester and leaves us dissatisfied.

Research confirms that social assertiveness tools have been helpful for many people in their personal lives. Such studies and meta-analyses have supported the notion that social skills–training involving assertiveness has helped reduce anxiety, particularly social anxiety, as well as enhance self-esteem and reduce depression.[1]

SOCIAL ASSERTIVENESS IS A BIG DEAL

Rosa Parks is not only an icon of the American civil rights movement, but she's also a powerful model of assertive behavior for all of us. Although quiet and shy by nature, she had also been taught by her grandfather to never accept herself as a second-class citizen. And she never did. Black Americans had lived through horrific centuries of slavery in the United States, only to be followed by horrific years of institutionalized oppression. When Parks was born in Alabama in 1913, Black people in the southern United States could not use the same hospitals, schools, restaurants, parks, or any other (much higher quality) facility that White people used. They could not live near White people or sit next to them (or in front of them) on buses. They were only allowed to have menial jobs, and their children were required to walk to school, while White children rode in buses. It was virtually impossible for Black citizens to register to vote and unthinkable for them to run for political office. This institutionalized White supremacy was enforced by laws, courts, police force, and by routine violence and lynching. It is very painful to imagine all this now, and deeply important to remember.

Parks lived within this world, but she did not accept it. As quiet and reserved as she was, in 1943, at age 30, she became active in the civil rights movement and was secretary of the local chapter of the NAACP (National Association for the Advancement of Colored People) in Montgomery. Progress for Black people was strongly resisted and immensely slow, and the daily indignities, humiliations, and intimidation continued. On December 1, 1955, when she was 42 years old, Parks decided that she had simply had enough. After a long day's work, when she was ordered by a bus driver to give up her seat to a White man, she refused.

> People always say that I didn't give up my seat because I was tired, but that isn't true. I was not tired physically, or no more tired than I usually was at the end of a working day. I was not old, although some people have an image of me as being old then. I was forty-two. No, the only tired I was, was tired of giving in.[2]

She was arrested by policemen and put in jail. But her simple, direct "no" that evening—and her determination—became pivotal in the civil rights movement. Black leaders and the Black community rallied behind this event, and within a week's time they had organized a citywide boycott of the bus system. In the process, these leaders elected a recently arrived, unknown 26-year-old minister, Martin Luther King Jr., to head the effort. It was hoped that the boycott might last at least one day, but instead it lasted 13 months, ending only when the US Supreme Court ruled against bus segregation. Many difficult and violent days were to come (King was killed just 13 years later), and Parks would receive death threats almost daily, but the civil rights movement had been launched in earnest.

Rosa Parks exemplified courageous and persistent assertiveness on both a personal and a societal basis. This chapter is mostly about everyday assertiveness to help us in our daily interactions with others. But the same basic principles apply to issues large and small, personal and societal.

During the 1970s and 1980s, assertiveness training began to play a more prominent role within cognitive behavioral therapy. In the 1970s, when the civil rights and women's rights movements were advancing further in the United States, a number of psychologists and researchers paid attention to assertiveness as a means of both protecting individual rights and enhancing personal well-being. References to assertiveness training in the academic literature peaked during this same time frame.

It is important to note that when it comes to issues of gender and ethnicity, at least in North America, the limited amount of extant research shows that both women and ethnic minorities in contemporary society are expressing themselves assertively, in ways that may have been very difficult (or even illegal) in times past. While research on these topics is sparse and somewhat contradictory, in the case of certain self-reporting data, both women and Black Americans rank higher than Caucasian males in terms of their assertive behavior, although there does not appear to be a clear statistical correlation between gender, ethnicity, and assertiveness.[3]

OUR CHALLENGE AS SOCIAL BEINGS

We humans are, by nature, social beings. Throughout history, we have lived in self-supporting groups: families, clans, tribes, villages, and nations. We instinctively care about the welfare of our groups and those close to us, and we also care about what our groups think of us. We have attachment needs, beginning in childhood. Many of the threats we feel in life come from other people: threats to our status, reputation, livelihood, sense of attachment, self-esteem, and safety. We instinctively don't want to look dumb, and we don't want to be disrespected, ridiculed, or looked down upon. We're wired this way. Many a battle has been fought over insults and saving face.

Unfortunately, our natural fear of not being accepted by other people can get in the way of expressing how we feel and what we want. Socrates compared the fear of others' opinions with a childhood fear of an imaginary boogeyman in the dark. In both cases, there is a nonphysical threat that nonetheless seems very real. Just as children can eventually learn to manage in the dark, despite their fears of a boogeyman, we adults can learn to express ourselves assertively, despite a natural fear of the opinions of others. We can still say the words, despite the pounding of our hearts. As Maggie Kuhn, the founder of the Gray Panthers (an activist group in support of the elderly), once said: "Speak your mind, even if your voice shakes."[4]

FUNCTIONAL ASSERTIVENESS

We likely carry around in our minds a stereotypical view of what an "assertive person" is, especially in the West. We might envision an individual who is bold, blunt, and outspoken—and maybe not too friendly. If this is our stereotype, then we cannot fully envision the assertiveness of people like Rosa Parks, Mahatma Gandhi, and Nelson Mandela, who were famous for being direct and persistent, but also civil and courteous. As a quiet Back woman in the Deep South of the United States in the 1950s, Parks did not fit within any stereotypical view of what a forceful and powerful person is. Yet this didn't matter. What matters with assertiveness is effectiveness.

Takashi Mitamura has used the term "functional assertiveness" to refer to applying forms of assertiveness that are best suited to specific social situations (including in different cultures).[5] It is only common sense that we would consider whether being more forceful or more friendly in our approach to assertiveness would lead to a more successful outcome in a given circumstance. Asserting oneself in a way that is normative in North America may be counterproductive in Asia and Latin America.[6] What may be perceived as acceptably candid and forcefully direct in one culture may be viewed as hostile in another. And, culture aside, we all intuitively know that direct and honest communication that is friendly and persuasive is more emotionally palatable than assertive pronouncements that are cold and demanding.

In Western cultures (particularly in the United States), some authors on the topic of assertiveness have taken the position that politeness and assertiveness do not go well together. But in many everyday situations, why should this be so? Mitamura makes the case for "pragmatic politeness," ascertaining which approach is most functionally appropriate for a given culture. As long as we arrive in the same place (i.e., achieving an acceptable outcome), why would it not be preferable to express ourselves in a way that has a better chance of preserving goodwill? The two of us take the position that it's entirely possible, and generally desirable, to be simultaneously assertive and respectful toward others. Why use a sledgehammer when a more delicate tool gets the same job done, with much less damage?

On the other hand, if your communication approaches are *not* effective in getting to desired outcomes, then functional assertiveness, as we define it, would dictate that more forceful, less friendly approaches be employed. Indeed, if we are dealing with belligerent or cruel people, this is likely the place to start. To that end, in this book we provide a tool kit that gives individuals a range of approaches that can be applied to match their unique personalities, circumstances, and culture—tools that can be either friendlier or less friendly.

We might think of functional assertiveness as a continuum. Assertive communication approaches represent a range of techniques, rather than a single point on the continuum (figure 1.1).

Some of the approaches discussed in this book sit a little to the left of the middle (they are more passive), and others lie a little to the right (they are more aggressive). Depending on the situation, you might choose to be somewhat more passive or more aggressive within the assertive range.

What is absolutely essential in any approach is that we still end up honestly expressing what we want and how we feel, and that we are persistent reaching an acceptable outcome, while also respecting the rights of others. The style of how we get there is only important in terms of its practical effectiveness. Often a more cooperative, friendly approach is a good place to start.

Figure 1.1 Communication continuum

A "BILL OF ASSERTIVE HUMAN RIGHTS"

Assertiveness is strengthened not only by learning new skills, but also by developing a strong, healthy, personal belief that we will not be a second-class citizen. We need to confirm our own set of core personal rights—rights that are not necessarily provided by laws or governments, but ones that we personally choose to give ourselves. This is central to self-determination. Arthur Lange and Patricia Jakubowski, early researchers in the field of assertiveness, once defined assertiveness as *standing up for personal rights and expressing thoughts, feelings, and beliefs in direct, honest, and appropriate ways that do not violate another person's rights*.[7] For them, assertiveness includes basics rights.

1. To have and express our needs.
2. To have feelings and express them.
3. To have opinions and express them.
4. To determine whether we want to meet the expectations of others.

All with the understanding that we respect similar rights for others.

In his pioneering book on assertiveness, *When I Say No, I Feel Guilty*, Manuel Smith provides an explicit list of what he defines as a "Bill of Assertive Human Rights."[8] Among these items are the simple rights to

- be the ultimate judge of ourselves and of what's best for us,
- offer no excuses,
- determine if we want to solve other people's problems,

- change our minds,
- make mistakes and be responsible for them,
- not need to be liked by others,
- say, "I don't know," and
- say, "I don't understand."

In particular, this list was developed to help people respond to manipulation and control by others, where individuals or institutions attempt to get us to do what they want by making us feel guilty, ignorant, or foolish. We have the basic right to be responsible for our own lives and let others be responsible for theirs, as long as harm is not being done to others. And we, of course, have a right to not be assertive at all, if we choose not to be!

While humanists and psychologists have come up with various lists of basic rights relating to assertiveness, they all tend to flow from a primary adult right: **I'm the ultimate judge of what's best for me**.

As an anchor for when we get into difficult situations with others, we can remind ourselves of this right, using it as a helpful personal compass. We can choose this right, even though it sometimes demands tremendous courage, and it can run the risk of extreme punishment in authoritarian social settings. Regarding his experience in a concentration camp during World War II, Viktor Frankl once wrote, "Everything can be taken from a man but one thing: the last of the human freedoms—to choose one's attitude in any given set of circumstances, to choose one's own way."[9] Even in much less extreme conditions, it can still require courage to choose one's own way, but the rewards are potentially life changing.

Without at least some assertiveness in our lives, we may end up conforming to what we think other people want us to be, rather than being our authentic selves. We are not fully who we are until we honestly express ourselves. We may not always get what we want, and there may be unanticipated, unpleasant consequences by exercising these rights. And we cannot force other people to change or agree with us. But we can determine and exercise our own set of personal assertiveness rights if we so choose.

In an interview in 2011 on CNN, Malala Yousafzai (the Pakistani women's and educational rights activist) identified the rights she believed a young female in this world should be able to claim for herself: the rights to participate in education, play, sing, talk, go to the market, and speak up.[10] This is not too much to ask for in our modern world.

What personal rights do you choose to claim for yourself?

FOUR CORE TOOLS OF SOCIAL ASSERTIVENESS FOR EVERYDAY LIVING

With the above discussion as background, let's take a look at specific social assertiveness tools that can be used in difficult everyday social interactions. Arnold Lazarus, a behavioral researcher and psychologist, once identified four core abilities to help people be more socially effective.[11]

1. Openly expressing one's desires and needs.
2. Saying no.
3. Expressing one's positive and negative emotions.
4. Adequately beginning, maintaining, and ending conversations.

Similar skills have been articulated by behavioral psychologists over time. In Scott's previous book for young people,

Speak Up and Get Along!, he compiled a set of tools that were based on the work of specialists in assertiveness training and behavioral psychology. Here are four core verbal skills that can help us directly express our needs, desires, and opinions, without the intent of rolling over other people.

Core Tool #1. *I*-Statements

As early as 1949, Andrew Salter recommended *I-statements* as a simple technique to help people express what they thought and felt. Salter did not specifically refer to this as "assertiveness training," but it was a means of seeking to help innately shy people express themselves more openly.[12] *I*-statements remain a key cornerstone of assertiveness. Directly expressing what we want and how we feel ensures that people clearly understand our point of view. It empowers our individuality. In particular, when people are being difficult, unkind, critical, or uncooperative, *I*-statements are the place to start when telling them exactly what we want and how we feel. Table 1.1 has some examples of *I*-statements.

Practicing *I*-statements in everyday interactions with people we know, on a friendly basis, can help us get used to the idea and prepare us for less friendly situations. If we're not used to this approach, it might initially be difficult emotionally for us to make direct statements to people. When we feel uncomfortable, one approach in helping us use *I*-statements is to employ honest and direct *self-disclosure*, affirming that this task is difficult. Self-disclosure—simply sharing our honest *feelings* in the moment with other people—can help as we learn to be more direct.

Here are some examples of using self-disclosure phrasing with *I*-statements when it's hard to be direct in our communications.

- "I don't like talking about this stuff, but I need to tell you how I feel."
- "I may be the only one who feels this way, but this is my opinion."
- "I hate to make it a big deal, but I really need your cooperation with this."
- "It's difficult for me to talk about a salary raise, but I feel like I need to."
- "Respectfully, I really feel differently."

Table 1.1 *I*-statements

Situation	*I*-statement response
Your spouse is talking over you without listening.	You: "I feel like you're not hearing what I'm saying."
A coworker is expressing a strong opinion about what needs to be done.	You: "I have a different opinion. I'd like to share what I think."
A supervisor is using belittling language to you.	You: "I understand that you're angry, but I really need to be treated like an adult."
A client is trying to get you to do something that is ethically questionable.	You: "I disagree. In good faith, I personally just can't do that."
A governmental or departmental administrator is trying to dismiss your concerns.	You: "I feel like you're not listening to me. I have a big problem here, and I need someone in your department, or your supervisor, to help."

I-statements are also crucial in our lives, to keep us from becoming manipulative toward others. In our roles as parents, siblings, neighbors, coworkers, and supervisors, we don't need to use blaming, guilt-inducing language in communicating with other people. We can simply express what we want and how we feel without trying to make others feel selfish, ignorant, or foolish. For example, parents can simply and directly say "I want you to . . . ," "I need you to . . . ," "I don't want you to . . . ," "I need to have you stop doing. . . . ," or "Please don't. . . ." We don't need to use guilt-inducing, belittling language, such as "You should know better" or "How could you?" or "I thought you were a big boy" or "What's your problem?"

Children can greatly benefit from parents who use an assertive parenting style, as opposed to parents falling back on bargaining, giving in, or manipulation. Children need both love and limits, and parents can help their children stay within reasonable behavioral boundaries by respectfully and directly expressing how they want and need their children to behave. And, as necessary, by communicating and following through on reasonable consequences if those requests are not met. Children also depend on their parents to be assertive in protecting them from the harmful behaviors of others.

Core Tool #2. No Thanks

It can be difficult to say *no thanks*, because of our innate desire to be liked by other humans. When people try to get us to do things we don't want to do, we may feel a measure of guilt in saying no. We might think that saying no will make us seem selfish, uncooperative, or no fun. When people need help and there's nobody else to offer it, there's good reason to jump in and help them. But there are also situations in life when we're asked to do things that people can readily accomplish themselves or when they just want our company in doing something they enjoy. When people try to get us to do things in their self-interest, we can equally—and without guilt—determine if their self-interest is more important than ours at that moment.

Saying no can be emotionally difficult, but doing so can be essential in setting boundaries and in self-care. Each of us needs to find our own comfortable phrasing for saying no in situations where it is hard for us to do so—particularly in saying no to bosses, parents, friends, siblings, coworkers, and love interests. As with *I*-statements, honest self-disclosure about the difficulty in saying no can be helpful.

There are many ways to express a comfortable no thanks.

- "Thanks for asking, but I'd better say no."
- "No, I'm sorry, but I can't."
- "I have to politely decline."
- "That won't fit into my schedule right now."
- "I feel bad about saying no, but I need to."
- "It's hard for me to say no, but I'm going to have to."
- "It sounds like fun, but I'll need to pass."
- "I'd better say no for now. I'll let you know if things change."
- "My loss, but I'd better say no."
- "No, no, a thousand times no!"

The musician Alicia Keys once wrote, "I began using the single most powerful word a pleaser can ever speak: No. It took practice. When pleasing has become your MO [modus operandi], it's tough to consistently begin holding your boundaries. But it gets easier the more you do it."[13] Think of saying no in pragmatic terms—that is, what works for you. It doesn't matter how we get to a no, as long as the outcome is functionally what we want. Eastern cultures often emphasize the importance of applying tact, politeness, respect, and gratitude as a means of preserving good relations and harmony. As long as we still end up stating what we need to express, this approach has the added benefit of maintaining cordial relationships in our very social world. The key is the outcome—*functional assertiveness*.

Core Tool #3. Simple Questions

In the same way that *I*-statements can help us express what we want and how we feel, asking *simple questions* can help us more assertively ask for what we want and need (including information). Simple questions are grounded in our assertive right to say, "I don't know" and "I don't understand." In line with these rights, we need to come to grips with the fact that we're not perfect. We don't know everything, we don't understand all things, we don't always listen or pay attention well, we get bored, and sometimes individuals don't explain things very well. People can also intentionally try to fool us or steamroll over us. We need to ask simple questions and not be intimidated until we get plain, clear answers, no matter how foolish or dumb we may feel. Table 1.2 has some examples of simple questions, including ones applying self-disclosure.

Peter Drucker, one of the world's leading organizational consultants, once said, "My greatest strength as a consultant is to be ignorant and ask a few questions."[14] Countries, businesses, and individuals have suffered dearly by someone not asking simple questions until they got reasonable answers. Why? Why not? What if . . . ? Why are we doing it this way? What if we don't do it at all? Is there a better way? What are the risks, and what are the costs? How do you (they) know this? What does that mean? Why does this matter?

The talk show host Larry King believed that the most important question was "Why?"[15] A why question helps test

Table 1.2 Simple questions

Situation	Simple question response
You're learning the tasks of a new job.	You: "I don't understand. Can you please explain?" or "I'm just not getting it. Can you go over it again?"
A mechanic is explaining why an expensive repair needs to be done.	You: "Can you go over the details and the cost of each item with me?" or "Is there a cheaper way to do this?"
A supervisor is explaining a new program.	You: "Just so I'm clear, why are we doing it this way? Won't this take more time and be less effective?"
A professor expresses a questionable opinion.	You: "How do you (they) know this?" or "Why would that be true?"
A sales assistant tries to add fees that were not previously disclosed.	You: "What are these fees about?" or "Why weren't they disclosed?" or "These seem wrong. Who can I talk to?"

assumptions and forces fuller explanations. If we feel foolish or dumb about asking a question, it's time to ask ourselves, "What's the worst that could happen by asking this question?" Asking seemingly dumb questions is a strength, not a weakness. This is how Larry King viewed it: "I ask dumb."

Core Tool #4. Persistence

Persistence is another cornerstone of assertiveness. Without it, assertive communications can be completely ineffective. Persistence means continuing to calmly repeat ourselves as often as we need to, until people recognize that we're not giving up until we achieve resolution. Difficult people, in both commercial and personal situations, sometimes count on blowing us off until we give up. Assertiveness is ineffective until we reach a reasonable outcome or at least have played out every card in our hand. Of course, in the case of dangerous social interactions, persistence is a bad idea, and we quickly need to disappear.

There are two important considerations in order to be effective when persisting in difficult situations.

1. Sometimes the person we're talking to might not be able to make a decision (e.g., a salesperson, work supervisor, government employee, or company representative). It does no good to continue to be persistent with them. They're simply carrying out someone else's wishes. If we find ourselves in this situation, persistence means going up the decision-making ladder ("I need to speak to the person who makes decisions" or "I need to appeal this, so who do I need to speak to?"), until we find and can express ourselves to the decision makers.
2. If we've gone up the decision-making ladder as far as we can go and still have not come to a satisfactory conclusion, then we need to find some form of referee (a mediator, court of law, advocacy association, etc.). Decision makers might hope that we will run out of steam, but if we're in the right, then we need not stop until every avenue has been assertively pursued.

Table 1.3 has some examples of persistence in assertive communications (with the idea that you would continue until reasonable satisfaction is obtained).

If we are pursuing significant, long-term objectives, only continued persistence and determination will be effective. Few people in modern history have been as assertively persistent as Mahatma Gandhi. For 32 years (between 1915 and 19470, from age 46 to 78, he tirelessly worked for India's independence. He spoke out, wrote extensively, and led

Table 1.3 Persistence

Situation	Persistence response
Other: "I need you to work on Saturday."	You: "I can't. I have other obligations this weekend."
Other: "This is really important; we may lose a customer if you don't."	You: "I really wish I could, but I can't."
Other: "Come on, we really need the help."	You: "I'm sorry, but I really can't. Is there some other way I can help before Saturday?"
Other: "We need the payment for our services now."	You: "I'm happy to pay you when the work we agreed to is completed."
Other: "The work is pretty much done.	You: "The agreement was that I'll pay you when it's 100 percent finished."
Other: "Please help us out with payment, since it's almost done."	You: "I really can't, but I'll pay you just as soon as it's all done."
Other: "I'm sorry, but we can't schedule an appointment for three months."	You: "This is really a serious situation, so that won't work."
Other: "I wish I could help, but we just don't have any other openings."	You: "Normally that might work for me, but not in this situation."
Other: "As I said, I wish I could do something, but I just can't."	You: "This just won't work, so we need to find a solution. Who can I talk to? Do I need to come there to discuss this?"

political and legal efforts. His approach was the epitome of assertiveness: besides speaking out, he engaged in noncooperation and civil disobedience with oppressive officials, but he did so with nonviolence. He led strikes, boycotts, marches, and fasts, and he was jailed seven times (13 times, including his earlier efforts in South Africa). He maintained that "noncooperation with evil is as much a duty as is cooperation with good,"[16] and he tenaciously stated that "until we win, we shall have to go on extending the scope of non-cooperation."[17] He was a gadfly and an irritant to the British Empire, since he persistently refused to go away. Throughout his life, Gandhi exemplified the power of his belief that "one has to speak out and stand up for one's convictions."[18]

* * * * *

In sum, these four core tools can be used in a broad variety of difficult social interactions. There are additional assertiveness tools, however, that can help with the following specific common difficulties.

1. Dealing with manipulation and rudeness.
2. Dealing with criticism.
3. Dealing with conflict.
4. Dealing with shyness.

Let's look at each difficulty, as well as the additional tools that can help.

SPECIFIC TOOLS FOR DEALING WITH MANIPULATION AND RUDENESS

One of the biggest challenges in human interactions is dealing with manipulation. *Manipulation* is an attempt to influence others by employing indirect, deceptive, or underhanded tactics. When people use guilt, fear, ridicule, cruelty, coercion, dishonesty, exaggeration, rejection, silence, or blame as a means of trying to get their way or making us feel bad, it is important to recognize and counter such manipulations, rather than simply giving in to them. Manipulation happens at all levels of society: in governments, businesses, and social and cultural institutions, as well as in everyday living among families, friends, employers, and merchants. With all of these levels of influence, it remains important to remind ourselves of our primary assertive right: *we are the ultimate judge of what's best for us*. This is a right that we should not hand over to *anyone*.

Rudeness runs the full gamut of belittling communication: from disrespect and insulting sarcasm to ridicule and cruelty. People typically use rudeness to blow off steam, manipulate, or inflict emotional pain. But the motivation doesn't matter if, as a result, you get treated as a second-class citizen. Instead, you can choose to respond assertively. The first place to start in addressing manipulation is with the four core assertiveness skills: *I*-statements, no thanks, simple questions, and persistence. *I*-statements and simple questions can be particularly useful in dealing with manipulation and rudeness. In these situations, politeness is fine if you want to give it a try, but it certainly is not needed and, perhaps, not even desirable.

Table 1.4 has some examples of *I*-statements in dealing with manipulation and rudeness. *I*-statements are also helpful when people ask us questions meant to demean or ridicule, rather than asking us sincere and honest questions (table 1.5).

Simple questions are another powerful tool in dealing with both manipulation and rudeness (table 1.6).

Below are some additional tools that can help us deal with manipulation and rudeness.

Shrugging

Sometimes, manipulation and rudeness are not worth our time. Rather than getting into a full-fledged discussion that will go nowhere, a verbal or nonverbal shrug may be sufficient. We can simply move along without making any comment, or we can use simple phrases.

- "Got it."
- "I've got to get going."
- "It just doesn't matter to me."
- "I just don't care."
- "Let's talk later."
- "That's a tough one."

Shrugging can be a profoundly powerful tool, but it's not easy to pull this off emotionally. Shrugging is particularly important in the early stages of incidental everyday outbursts: potential road rage, unreasonable customers, and the like. If

Table 1.4 *I*-statements in dealing with manipulation and rudeness

Situation	*I*-statement response
Other: "Get your big butt out of that chair and get some work done."	You: "Please don't talk to me that way. There's no need to ridicule me."
Other: "I've told you a thousand times that you need to dress better for these kinds of events."	You: "These clothes are completely appropriate for this event, and I would like you to please be respectful."
Other: "I thought you would know all this stuff a lot better, with all your education and big resumé."	You: "I want to have a respectful discussion, so let's get together another time when we can do so."
Other: "I've sacrificed everything for this family. And this is the gratitude I get? I just don't know what I'm going to do next."	You: "I see that you're upset, but I need to be able to talk about this without guilt or threats. Let's just sit down, talk about it in some detail, and see if we can find a solution" or "Let's table this for later, when we're able to discuss it calmly."

Table 1.5 I-statements in dealing with questions

Situation	I-statement response
Other: "That was really stupid. Why did you do that?"	You: "Because I wanted to."
Other: "Why are you wearing those clothes?"	You: "Because I like them."
Other: "How could you do that?"	You: "Because I made a mistake."
Other: "What were you thinking?"	You: "Apparently, I was not thinking in the way you believe I should have."

Table 1.6 Simple questions in dealing with manipulation and rudeness

Situation	Simple question response
Other: "I'd like to promote you, but you're not ready yet."	You: "Why do you think I'm not ready?"
Other: "Well, you just need more experience."	You: "What experience do I need?"
Other: "Probably just more technical experience."	You: "What, exactly? If I get that experience, do I get the promotion?"
Other: "It's incredible that you would do such a dumb thing."	You: "What's incredible about it?"
Other: "It's just in really bad taste."	You: "What's in bad taste about it?"
Other: "It probably insulted a lot of people."	You: "Why would they be insulted? If they were insulted, what can I do about it?"
Other: "I'll never forgive you for talking to me that way."	You: "What did I say?"
Other: "You said you were disappointed because of how I treated Mom."	You: "I honestly felt that way at the time, but what can we do now to make this better?
Other: "Nothing."	You: "Why not?"

danger is involved, then avoidance is crucial. *Avoidance* is getting out of a situation we perceive as dangerous, whereas shrugging is determining that an interaction is not worth our time or attention.

Maybe-Phrasing

In dealing with difficult, manipulative people, if we find that some of what they say might be accurate, but what they're really trying to do is use ridicule or guilt to vent emotions or get their own way, *maybe*-phrasing can be effective. *Maybe*-phrasing (similar to what Manuel Smith called "fogging") means using persistent, noncommittal, conditional phrasing to counter manipulation. Similar to shrugging, after using *maybe*-phrasing, we can just move on. *Maybe*-phrasing involves wording such as "Maybe," "Could be," "That might be true," "You could be right," "Possibly," and "Who knows."

Table 1.7 has some examples of using *maybe*-phrasing in dealing with manipulation and rudeness. *Maybe*-phrasing can be especially helpful in answering questions that are meant to demean (table 1.8). Such phrasing leaves others with little else to say and thus does not reward manipulation.

You-Statements

From time to time, we need to teach people—perhaps quite impolitely—how we want to be treated. Sometimes domineering, manipulative individuals have gotten into a habit of speaking to people in whatever way they please, thinking that they can do this to everyone who gets in their way. In those situations, shrugging and *maybe*-phrasing may not feel like strong enough responses. *I*-statements are clearly one effective means to express what we think and how feel in any situation. But with people who are habitually hostile and manipulative—and

Table 1.7 *Maybe*-phrasing in dealing with manipulation and rudeness

Situation	*Maybe*-phrasing response
Other: "That stuff you tweeted yesterday was pretty ridiculous."	You: "You might be right."
Other: "For sure. I thought you were smart, but now I know differently."	You: "You think so?"
Other: "Absolutely."	You: "Could be.
Other: "That was one of the dumbest things I've seen anybody do."	You: "Could be."
Other: "You surprised even me with that one."	You: "Clearly."
Other: "You certainly did."	You: "You might be right."
Other: "Can't you think of anybody besides yourself?"	You: "Maybe not."
Other: "And then you're a smart aleck on top of it."	You: "Maybe."
Other: "What an idiot."	You: "Maybe."

Table 1.8 *Maybe*-phrasing in dealing with questions

Situation	*Maybe*-phrasing response
Other: "Aren't you acting a little childish?"	You: "Maybe."
Other: "Why would you ever do such a thing?"	You: "I'm not sure."
Other: "When are you going to get your act together?"	You: "Maybe someday."

use ridicule and name calling as a weapon—we can also employ very direct *you-statements* to point out the absurdity and childishness of what they're saying and place all the attention and onus back on them. Table 1.9 has some of examples of using *you*-statements to do this.

Table 1.9 *You*-statements to point out absurdity and rudeness

Situation	You-statement response
Other: "You're an idiot for voting for that candidate."	You: "You've got to be kidding me. You actually talk to people this way?"
Other: "You're a real loser. Do you know that?"	You: "You've got serious issues you need to work through. In the meantime, either speak to me respectfully or let's not talk."
Other: "You people are all alike. Just lazy as hell."	You: "I can't believe you could possibly speak to another person that way. What's your problem?"
Other: "You're just a young guy, but you come in here talking like you know everything."	You: "Seriously? This is how you talk to people who are younger than you? You really need to listen and then see what you think, rather than judging people from the start."
Other: "My mother was completely right about you. You're an idiot, and I should never have gotten involved with you."	You: "Why do you have to be so mean? Just tell me how you want to resolve this, without all the meanness."

* * * * *

In sum, the unfortunate reality is that there are hostile, manipulative people in the world. And sometimes even mostly nice people can have emotional outbursts, where they say rude things that they later regret. This is all *part of life*. But we should not be friends with anyone who is consistently mean, cruel, or abusive to us or others. In research on bullying prevention, there is the very sad phenomenon of bullied young people seeking out approval, acceptance, and even friendship from the person who is chronically bullying them. Their hope is that they can turn the painful rejection of the bullying person into acceptance. Similar behavior is sometimes found among adults who experience domestic violence. All of us, whether child or adult, need to get out of relationships with people who are consistently mean, cruel, or abusive. Life is too short to spend any more time than we need to with chronically unkind people.

Responding to Rudeness on the Internet

All of the tools that have been described in this chapter also apply to interacting with rude and manipulative people on the internet. The challenge is that once our communications are made in the digital world, they can be copied and shared, thus taking on a life of their own. So it's vitally important to have some restraint in what we post, including in how we respond to others. Do we really want the words or images we post to be shared with the world, as well as to have an indefinite life on the internet?

If someone posts something that is mean or cruel, our first step is to decide whether to shrug it off or stop further communications with this person (including potentially blocking that individual). If it's someone we care about or can't simply walk away from (e.g., a family member or co-worker), we can try to communicate with that person directly, by a text or email. Often a phone conversation is even better, as it allows a back-and-forth discussion. It's harder to be mean in a one-on-one personal discussion. Alternatively, we can try *maybe*-phrasing and *you*-statements, if we have the discipline to stop after a single exchange. We don't want to get into a battle with them, so the key is then to either cease responding or block the other party. If interactions become threatening, it can be important to (1) report the threats to the sponsoring company or moderator of the site,

(2) keep a copy of threatening messages, and (3) contact law enforcement.

This book is about using assertive tools to enhance our well-being. Of course, the much larger question is how much social media interaction is really good for our well-being. There is growing evidence that social media use can increase anxiety, particularly among young people.[19]

SPECIFIC TOOLS FOR DEALING WITH CRITICISM

It's easy to feel defensive when we're criticized. It can seem like we're somehow diminished if we make a mistake and then are told about it. Blame can feel like a threat. This is further complicated by the fact that sometimes criticism and blame become emotional outbursts or are used as manipulative tools, rather than simply as a means of trying to correct something. Criticism can make us feel vulnerable and foolish. How we respond assertively depends on whether the criticism is accurate.

Mea Culpa

If the criticism is completely or mostly correct, assertiveness calls for responsibly agreeing with it and making up for any harm (e.g., "I agree, that was a mistake" or "You're right, I'll do better next time" or "Yes, that was not good; I apologize, so what can I do to make up for it?"). *Mea culpa* means "my fault" in Latin, and a clear, direct admission of mea culpa is always the most assertive thing to do when the blame is accurate. But a mea culpa doesn't just involve saying something directly. It also means taking responsibility for a mistake and making up for it as best we can. There's no need to get defensive when criticism is mostly accurate. We simply have to own

Table 1.10 Mea culpa statements

Situation	Mea culpa response
Other: "You really screwed up. You were supposed to get that package sent out yesterday."	You: "You're right, that was a screwup. I'm sorry, and I'll get it sent out today."
Other: "You were supposed to be home two hours ago. You've messed up my whole day."	You: "You're right, I messed up. How can I make it up to you?"
Other: "You can't make up for it. It was just very selfish."	You: "You're right. It was selfish. I apologize."
Other: "It was totally unreasonable to yell at me like that."	You: "You're completely right. I lost my cool, and I apologize. I'll try to do better."
Other: "That joke you texted was completely inappropriate."	You: "You're right. That was really dumb of me. It won't happen again."

up to the mistake and assertively agree that it was a problem. Table 1.10 has examples of the mea culpa tool.

No Way

On the other hand, if the criticism directed at us is completely or mostly incorrect, it's just as important to respond directly in those situations. Sometimes we take the path of least resistance by sloughing things off, assuming that we're dealing with difficult people who won't believe us anyway. This is a mistake. Even if they're unreasonable, they need to hear the truth. If we don't set the record straight, people may assume that our silence is an indication of guilt, and inaccurate impressions can be formed that can work against us in the future. When blame is incorrect, we need to assertively counter such blame each and every time (e.g., "No, that's simply not true; this is what happened" or " I don't agree; this is where you're wrong" or "I'm sorry, but that's not true. The

Table 1.11 No-way statements

Situation	No-way response
Other: "You really didn't use your best effort on this one."	You: "It might not have been obvious, but I actually did put in a really strong effort. How could I have done better?"
Other: "You tried to take money from Dad and Mom that was meant for me."	You: "That's completely false. If you want to take the time to understand, I can explain why. But it's totally false, regardless of who tells you otherwise."
Other: "I saw you flirting with that guy. What's your problem?"	You: "I can guarantee you that it is 100 percent false. But let's talk about this, so I can understand why you would think that way."
Other: "It's pretty clear that you went behind my back on this one and talked to others."	You: "I can see how it might look that way, but it's just not true. Let me explain."

truth is . . ."). It's just as important to clear up any blame that we don't deserve as it is to take responsibility when we do merit it. Examples of the *no way* tool appear in table 1.11.

Of course, setting the record straight should only be done if what we're saying is completely true. If we're not entirely truthful, then we will eventually pay for it by not being trusted in the future. It's much better say "mea culpa" or explain something in detail if a statement is only partly true, rather than develop a reputation for unreliability and dishonesty. Direct, honest communication is at the core of verbal assertiveness.

SPECIFIC TOOLS FOR DEALING WITH CONFLICT

Conflicts, both large and small, are a basic part of human life. It's quite natural for people to desire different things, and if both parties feel strongly about what they want, conflict is sometimes the result. It's understandable that we have arguments from time to time, but habitual arguments that become personal attacks can be very destructive to relationships. Fortunately, we are also endowed with problem-solving abilities. We can identify problems and develop workable solutions. When conflicts occur, sometimes both parties tenaciously hold onto what they want (their positions), in the hope that the other party will give in or solve the problem for them. The most assertive thing we can do in a conflict situation is to provide leadership by initiating and offering solutions.

Workable Solutions

Early on in their marriage, Scott's grandparents established an exemplary tradition of sitting down at the kitchen table and talking things through when they had disagreements. Rather than going on and on with unhelpful arguments and holding tight to their positions, they developed a conscious practice of settling down (the physical act of sitting down together helped) and going through informal discussion and problem solving. Given our emotional state during disagreements, it's not easy to pull this off. But in the end, *workable solutions* require some form of the involved parties sitting down to express what they want and how they feel, as well as asking simple questions to make sure there's clarity about the problem and each person's point of view. In our most important personal relationships, it's especially crucial to break out of emotionally driven patterns of conflict and stay in the mode of seeking a workable solution.

Assertive leadership in resolving everyday disagreements can be launched by solution-focused statements.

- "Let's sit down and write out our options."
- "Here's what I think we should do. What do you think?"
- "I'm responsible for this decision, but I'd like the benefit of your perspective and ideas before I make it."
- "Can we simply take turns on this or make a list of who does what?"
- "I'm busy right now, but can we meet in an hour to resolve the problem?"
- "This could get emotional, so let's sit down and compare our perspectives."
- "We have a big difference of opinion on this, so why don't we bring in outside advice to help us decide?"

The Harvard Negotiation Project was jointly founded by Roger Fisher and William Ury. Its objective was to determine the best elements of principled conflict resolution and negotiation. The project resulted in *Getting to Yes* and subsequent publications.[20] The key principles of conflict resolution coming out of the Harvard Negotiation Project apply to conflicts big and small. The following are a few of its main principles

- *Separate the people from the problem*: Strive to understand the other party's perceptions and feelings about the issue (the human element). Be hard on the problem and soft on the person.
- *Focus on interests, rather than positions*: Focus less on *what* you each want (your positions) and more on *why* you want it (your interests). This can lead to new solutions.

- *Create options for mutual gain*: Come up with multiple ideas that can satisfy at least some of the interests for each party (*win-win solutions*).
- *Don't allow power plays or game playing*: If it becomes clear that you're dealing with a bad-faith party, either get a referee (a mediator, judge, or counselor) or walk away with whatever result best meets your own interests.

While the principles developed by Fisher and Ury apply to more formal negotiations, they also can be used in everyday disagreements, as well as for conflicts in general.

Negotiations are much quicker and more effective when there is mutual goodwill, supported by objective information, rather than an agreement simply based on trust. It can be quite beneficial to do enough research to obtain objective information and determine what's fair for both sides. This information can include financial survey data, ideas from experts in a field, and researched ideas on what a win-win solution might look like. Again, these basic ideas apply to both organizational and interpersonal disagreements.

Cool Down

We all have an innate emotional thermostat when it comes to conflict. Nonetheless, our emotions can be much quicker and more powerful than our reasoning faculties. And some of us feel frustrated and angry more quickly than others. This is one of those cases where following Socrates's admonition to "know thyself" is quite important. If we have a tendency to quickly say or do things out of anger that we might later regret, then stopping and *cooling down* can be very important. We can use direct self-disclosure, such as "I'm starting to feel angry, and

I might say some things I will regret," or simply say, "Let's take a break and talk a little later." If this happens in public and involves something like potential road rage or another serious confrontation with someone we don't know, it's particularly important to walk (or drive) away and cool down. Any time real danger is involved, getting away is not simply an effort to cool down, but a means to protect ourselves and others.

SPECIFIC TOOLS FOR DEALING WITH SHYNESS

Another important aspect of social assertiveness is being able to develop positive social relationships and friendships, if we want to. *Shyness*—feeling uncomfortable, self-conscious, or worried around others—can get in the way. There is not a lot of statistical data on adult shyness, but in a 2019 YouGov survey in the United Kingdom, 57 percent of the survey respondents considered themselves to be shy (47 percent as "somewhat shy" and 10 percent as "very shy").[21]

We are all innately different when it comes to sociability. Some people are gregarious and talkative, while others are much less so. If we tend toward introversion, it may not mean that we are shy. Instead, we may need quietness or alone time to recharge our social batteries. We may be more selective and deliberate in our social interactions and, therefore, possibly more naturally restrained. At a dinner party, one of the guests told American president Calvin Coolidge, nicknamed "Silent Cal" for his lack of interest in chitchat, that she had bet a friend she could get him to say more than five words. His response was "You lose."

Happiness research suggests that at least a few close and loving relationships are important for our well-being. And good relationships with people can enhance our everyday lives at home, at work, and in our general interactions with the public. If we are easily frustrated with people or have a more private or shy personality, being around people may simply not be as enjoyable. And this is fine. But if we want to actively broaden or strengthen relationships, there are three verbal skills that we can use in friendly social situations.

Investigative Questions

When it's difficult to find words to maintain a conversation, ask *investigative questions*. Become a detective, like Sherlock Holmes. Moreover, this process can go beyond merely asking simple questions. It also involves the use of authentic, *open-ended questions*, in order to really understand a person and the interests and activities in that individual's life. It means putting ourselves aside for a moment and *mindfully* placing our focus on and interest in another human being. Try the following:

- Open-ended questions that don't elicit just a yes or no response.
- Reflective listening, either by repeating what we think we've heard or simply saying, "Tell me more."
- Follow-up questions.
- Genuine concern and sympathy.

Closed-ended questions also can lead to follow-up questions, so there's no need to get technical. The key is simply to ask questions. There are many questions we can ask that not only break the ice but that can also be fun to explore with others.

- "What have you been doing lately?"
- "What's your opinion about . . . ?"

- "What's your favorite (food, movie, hobby, sports team, vacation spot, smart phone app, etc.)?"
- "How do you feel about (an interesting event or issue in the news)?"
- "What upcoming plans do you have?"
- "What do you think about (whatever topic is being discussed)?

Using the phrase "Tell me more" as a follow-up to an answer can always prompt further conversation.

Asking investigative questions is one of those skills that can become an ongoing, bridge-building habit if consciously applied. Begin with those closest to you and move outward from there. Examples of investigative questions appear in table 1.12.

Table 1.12 Investigative questions

Closed-ended question	Open-ended question
Do you like your job?	How do you like your job? What's best about it?
Where did you go on your vacation?	How was your vacation? What did you do?
Did you watch the Academy Awards ceremony last night	How did you like the Academy Awards ceremony last night?

Self-Disclosure

As described earlier, *self-disclosure* can help us be more direct and honest in our communications (e.g., "It's hard for me to tell you this" or "I hate to make this a big deal"). Self-disclosure can also be useful in building relationships, such as by openly and honestly sharing how we feel and what we think, as well as recounting our life experiences and interests. This also increases our understanding of others and their experiences. In particular, it means being authentic and nondefensive in communicating both positive and negative aspects of our lives. Being open and honest not only frees us up by not having to protect our self-image, but it also reinforces healthy self-acceptance, regardless of the foibles, fears, and uncertainties in our lives. Honest transparency inspires rapport, trust, and connections with others. People are more likely to be willing to recount information about their lives if we step forward and candidly share something from ours. Honestly expressing our appreciation of and love for someone close to us fosters further closeness.

Here are further examples of self-disclosure.

- "I think I know exactly how you feel. I once had the same thing happen."
- "I don't know how you had the guts to do that. It would have been supremely difficult for me."
- "To tell you the truth . . ."
- "I'm OK in some areas but not so good at what you're talking about, either."
- "If it'll make you feel better, let me share this little gem with you."
- "I feel uncomfortable in these kinds of situations. How about you?"
- "I know I'm way out of the mainstream, but this is what I think about that."

Kind Communication

The power of *kind communication* in interactions is discussed further in chapter 3, but let it just be said here that if we don't engage in at least some level of respectful and kind communication with others, we might as well forget about building relationships. Kindness is the glue of human society. Providing compliments, encouragement, sympathy, and positive suggestions can develop bonds of goodwill. But verbal communication is only one way of conveying kindness, and nonverbal forms can be even more powerful. Other meaningful ways of communicating kindness and building relationships are sharing; helping others with chores and physical labor; being with someone during difficult times; doing favors; giving gifts; and eating, talking, or walking together. No matter how shy we may innately feel, we can communicate kindness in both verbal and nonverbal ways.

SHYNESS VERSUS SOCIAL ANXIETY

There is quite a bit of overlap between shyness and social anxiety, but the latter involves more than just shyness. *Social anxiety* is one of the most prevalent psychological challenges. It typically begins early in life, is persistent and long lasting (because few people seek treatment for this affliction, and it has a low natural recovery rate), and creates a significant functional disability in one's daily life.

Although the relationship between shyness and social anxiety remains unclear, some researchers have hypothesized that both conditions exist on the same continuum, with social anxiety being conceptualized as "extreme shyness."[22] This means that shyness and social anxiety share many features. They both have an emotional dimension (fear and anxiety), a physical dimension (e.g., trembling, sweating, blushing), and a mental dimension (e.g., fear of negative evaluations). Nonetheless, it's clear that, in comparison with shy people, those with social anxiety are more impaired by their severe symptoms of distress and avoidance of social situations.

Many people don't realize that there are differences between shyness and social anxiety, which may lead to the latter symptom being brushed off, and people not getting the help they need. Shyness can sometimes develop into social anxiety if, over time, it results in someone habitually avoiding, worrying about, or analyzing social interactions. Table 1.13 summarizes key differences between shyness and social anxiety.

Previous research indicates that people with social anxiety take longer to seek treatment once their symptoms begin, compared with other anxiety disorders.[23] Common reasons for this are assuming social anxiety problems are part of their personality (e.g., shyness, introversion), being afraid of what others (including health care professionals) might think or say about them if they seek treatment, having financial barriers, or simply being unsure of where to go for help.[24]

Table 1.13 Shyness versus social anxiety

Characteristic of shyness	Characteristic of social anxiety
Shy people may feel uncomfortable in social situations, but they can usually motivate themselves to perform or behave in a friendly way when necessary.	People with social anxiety tend to avoid social situations or undergo intense anxiety when participating in them, which can affect their work, schooling, and other daily activities.
Shy people have a remarkable potential to get rid of their shyness when they mature or when they get used to an unfamiliar social situation or unfamiliar people.	People with social anxiety may either remain unchanged or get worse, even when they become used to an unfamiliar social situation or unfamiliar people.
Shyness is a personality trait that doesn't require treatment.	Social anxiety is a mental challenge that requires treatment.

The good news is that social anxiety is highly treatable and manageable. The most common forms of therapy involve counseling (including psychotherapy), medications, or both. Clinical practice guidelines in the United Kingdom specifically recommend cognitive behavioral therapy as the first line of treatment for social anxiety.[25] In Naoki's previous research, this was an effective treatment option for people with social anxiety, even for those who had not responded to the use of prescription drugs.[26] Furthermore, in recent years you can access cognitive behavioral therapy resources via the internet in some places and countries.[27] It's time to seek treatment for social anxiety if you have been severely distressed, avoid social situations, and thus have difficulty functioning normally in your daily life.

As families and organizations, we can all help reduce the magnitude of social anxiety by fostering and supporting honest, respectful self-expression. For example, in a cross-cultural study undertaken in 2010, researchers determined that people living in collectivistic East Asian cultures, where group harmony is encouraged through being submissive and quiet, reported higher social anxiety than those in individualistic Western cultures. This study also found, however, that people living in collectivistic Latin American cultures, where group harmony is pursued through being sociable, friendly, and talkative, reported a lower amount of social anxiety than those in both East Asian and Western cultures.[28]

TRAUMA AND SOCIAL ASSERTIVENESS

Some people may find it difficult to initiate direct and honest (i.e., assertive) communication with others, due to traumatic memories. They may have been subjected to serious bullying or habitual negative criticism from parents or other family members as they grew up, or they could have experienced serious physical or mental abuse. These memories can cripple people through negative images of themselves, the troubled emotions that accompany this view of themselves, and significant fear when interacting with people in general. Negative self-images can be intrusive and powerful, grab all of our attention, and stay with us in unsettling ways. Research shows that people who have social anxiety often experience recurrent negative self-images while interacting socially, and these images can be grounded in their early traumatic memories.[29]

This book is a self-help book, and we strongly recommend that if you have had seriously difficult or traumatic events in your life that contribute to anxiety, depression, and an inability to communicate with others in assertive ways, you should move beyond self-help and seek professional assistance. Talk to your medical doctor and get a referral to mental health professionals who have had experience in effectively working with trauma.

Professional efforts may involve some form of *imagery rescripting*, which is an experiential therapeutic technique that uses imagery and imagination to transform and reinterpret intrusive memories. It involves working with the mental images themselves, rather than just talking about these traumatic events. This method was initially developed for individuals experiencing post-traumatic stress disorder, or PTSD, but it has since been used to treat a broad variety of mental health problems, including social anxiety disorder, obsessive-compulsive disorder, bulimia nervosa, nightmare disorder, and personality disorders.[30] Imagery rescripting typically involves the following steps.[31]

1. Identifying the negative image and the key memories that are linked to it.
2. Clearly seeing the differences between *then* (you in your memory) and *now* (you today) by looking at this from an objective adult perspective, rather than from a lingering childhood point of view.
3. Replacing (i.e., rescripting) your negative image with a more realistic one, showing how you come across to others today.

SUMMARY OF TOOLS IN THIS CHAPTER

Four Core Tools

I-**statements**: clearly expressing what we want and how we feel.

No thanks: getting comfortable with saying no.

Simple questions: asking questions, even when we feel foolish doing so.

Persistence: not giving up until we arrive at an acceptable outcome.

Specific Tools for Dealing with Manipulation and Rudeness

Shrugging: not giving rude people the reaction they want.

Maybe-**phrasing**: neither agreeing nor disagreeing with manipulation and rudeness.

You-**statements**: putting the full focus back on manipulative and rude behavior.

Specific Tools for Dealing with Criticism

Mea culpa: if the criticism is correct, agreeing with it.
No way: if the criticism is incorrect, not sloughing it off, but verbally correcting it.

Specific Tools for Dealing with Conflict

Workable solutions: sitting down and working through the interests (not just the positions) behind the conflict.
Cool down: taking a break from emotionally charged or dangerous situations.

Specific Tools for Dealing with Shyness

Investigative questions: asking friendly, open-ended questions in a conversation.
Self-disclosure: opening up and sharing personal experiences, opinions, and foibles.
Kind communication: offering kind words and help.

CHAPTER 2

Jumping In

Behavioral Assertiveness

If we wait until we *feel* like doing something, we may never do it. We define behavioral assertiveness as *initiating needful or desired intentional activities, even when we don't feel like it*. Our natural instincts and unpleasant emotions can be obstacles to getting things done. Additionally, social pressures may keep us from engaging in activities that bring us satisfaction and enjoyment. An assertive alternative to avoidance behavior or traveling down paths that we don't personally value is *jumping in* with an activity of our own choosing.

Our thoughts can influence our emotions and behavior, but, just as clearly, behavior can impact thoughts and feelings. When we do something fun, when we finish a useful task, or when we help others, we often experience positive thoughts and emotions. On the other hand, when we have too much drudgery in our lives, too much inactivity, or too much confrontation with others, we most likely will experience negative emotions. Even simple physical activity, in and of itself (e.g., walking, physical labor, exercising), has been found to benefit our moods and mental health. Multiple studies have found a strong link between physical exercise and reduced anxiety or depression.[1]

BEHAVIORAL ACTIVATION

The technical term for jumping in and doing things, especially when we don't feel like it, is *behavioral activation*. This isn't always easy to do, and that's why jumping in is an intentional act of assertiveness. Ongoing research, particularly since the 1990s, suggests that formal behavioral activation can be even more effective in dealing with depression than purely cognitive approaches (i.e., mentally countering negative thoughts).[2] A major study in 2006 found that behavioral activation was as effective as an antidepressant drug (paroxetine) in dealing with depression.[3]

There are lots of things we need to do in life, such as contributing to the household income, taking care of family, carrying out daily chores, and solving both large and small problems at home and at work. Additionally, once our basic needs are taken care of, there are activities we often want to pursue, in order to add meaning and enjoyment to our lives (e.g., relationships, education, causes, hobbies, spirituality, etc.). To engage in these activities, we sometimes need to be willing to accept our moods and emotions at the current moment. We can't wait for them to be just right. Both pleasant and unpleasant feelings are a regular part of life, and it's important to not let the unpleasant ones impede us.

Behavioral psychologists tell us that following this pathway can be especially important if we become immobilized by fear or worry. When people have excessive, persistent sadness or low moods (i.e., depression), a natural, instinctive response is to slow down and be less active. If this inactive behavior goes on for too long, however, it can lead to deeper depression. These negative emotions and corresponding behaviors can be triggered by difficult events (e.g., losing a job, physical ailments, financial problems, loss of a loved one). They can also be due to natural genetic tendencies. Whatever the cause, one coping strategy, beyond getting professional medical attention as needed, is to start being active. When some people feel down or have low moods, their default behavior is to shut down, stay home, and not engage with others. Behavioralists suggest a different, more intentional approach—getting active, getting out, and getting help.

Abraham Lincoln is known not only for his exceptional leadership during the American Civil War but also for his inclination towards sadness and melancholy. His life was filled with difficult challenges, including unsettling emotions. He experienced poverty, the death of his mother when he was just 9 years old, the deaths of two young sons, and many political defeats (up until his election as president), not to mention the rejection of many of his fellow citizens when he was elected president, as well as the tragedies of a violent civil war. There is evidence that he inherited a family tendency toward depression. Despite all this, Lincoln is an astonishing example of continuing to jump in, even in the midst of dark circumstances and painful emotions. He continued to try new jobs; became a self-taught, successful lawyer; married and raised a family; and persisted in running for political office, even after defeats. Most importantly for the United States as a country, he remained actively engaged in his momentous responsibilities and efforts, even in the midst of his personal suffering. In the 1840s, Lincoln included this important bit of wisdom in a letter: "A tendency to melancholy . . . let it be observed, is a misfortune, not a fault."[4] And he once wrote, "Determine that the thing can and shall be done and then . . . find the way."[5]

Lincoln was an exceptional human being in many ways—we don't need to compare ourselves to him—and we cannot know exactly what level of depression he went through. Yet we do know that for a period of time, he could not get out of bed, due to "melancholy." We don't choose these unpleasant and painful emotions that naturally flow through us, and living with them can be one of life's biggest challenges. There are no easy answers. But the general lesson from Lincoln applies to our own everyday pursuits: our lives and the lives of others can benefit when we are able to jump into needful and desired activities in the midst of unpleasant emotions. This can be a very difficult task, and we need to go easy on ourselves if it's not always doable on any given day.

Action Precedes Motivation

Behavioralists tell us that we're more likely to act ourselves into feeling, instead of feel ourselves into action. Activity can breed further activity, and sometimes inactivity results in more inactivity. In other words, action often creates motivation, rather than vice versa.

"Vegging out" can be recharging. Doing less can sometimes make life more enjoyable. But if we find ourselves chronically avoiding necessary activities, due to the emotional discomforts and pain that naturally come with challenges in life, we need to consider activating behaviors. The raw sensations of unpleasant emotions are difficult enough, but the problem is compounded when those sensations keep us from engaging in needful and valued activities. Jumping in can generate internal motivation. It's working from the outside in. Regardless of whether our actions immediately result in motivation, if we jump in, our emotions will not have the same restrictive power over our lives. We can still accomplish the tasks of everyday living.

We've all been in a situation where something important needs to get done at work, and we convince ourselves that we'll do something about it when we feel more like it . . . perhaps tomorrow. And maybe we will. But if the tomorrows keep coming and going and we're still telling ourselves the same thing, it may be time to simply jump in. The liberation that comes with jumping in is that we don't need to feel like doing something, we just do it. We shut our eyes, plunge into the chilly waters of action, and start swimming. Often, all it takes to jump in is to commit ourselves to just a small part of a task. Then momentum usually takes over, and we can finish more than we initially set out to do.

If our emotions are overwhelming, behavioral activation means getting the professional help we need, just as we would with overwhelming physical pain. There is evidence that behavioral activation can be helpful in managing depression, and other approaches have also proven useful, including therapy and medication. Reaching out to health care professionals can help us in determining a good combination of approaches for our individual needs.

Passive versus Active Rest

In his clinical experience, Naoki has found that sometimes clients misunderstand the meaning and benefits of rest—that is, they don't know how to get the proper kinds of rest in specific situations. One of his clients, suffering from depression, said that his medical doctor had advised him to take a medication and get plenty of rest. So for two months, the client had been trying to lie in bed as much as possible, in order to get "plenty of rest" and not go outside. Naoki then explained the therapeutic difference between passive and active rest. *Passive rest* requires little to no expenditure of energy (e.g., sleeping, napping) and allows the body to repair cells, consolidate memories, and release growth hormones. It is important for our physical health, mental functioning, and emotional balance. On the other hand, *active rest* (initiated by behavioral activation) involves engaging in restorative, low-intensity activities, such as walking, reading for pleasure, cycling, and drawing. It's about refreshing ourselves by switching gears physically and mentally, changing our focus, and soothing our minds. Active rest is often preferred when trying to overcome a depressed mood. Understanding the symbiosis between passive and active rest allows us to tap into the full power of restful practices.

THREE TOOLS FOR FOSTERING BEHAVIORAL ACTIVATION

In the following sections, we explain three skill-set strategies that can help us in activating our behavior.

Tool #1. *But*-Twists

One of the major obstacles to taking action comes in the form of exaggerated "I can't" thoughts: "I can't," "It's too hard," "I don't feel like it," or "I'm just too lazy." These kinds of thoughts and their corresponding emotions come to all of us. They're part of being human. But we also have the mental ability to intentionally counter those thoughts, in order to help us jump into activities when we really want or need to do so. Developing a repertoire of go-to rebuttals for such thoughts can help us get started.

In Scott's books for young people, he referred to these phrases as *but-twists*. A *but*-twist means responding to words that foster helplessness, such as countering "applying for this job is just too hard" with a constructive "*but* . . ." phrase. In this instance, some *but*-twists would be "*but* I can just get started" or "*but* it won't kill me" or "*but* it could make a big difference for me." The point of a *but*-twist is to use a few quick words to get us started. Here are some additional examples:

". . . *but* I can do it."
". . . *but* it's really not that hard."
". . . *but* it really won't take very long."
". . . *but* I can just take one small step at a time."
". . . *but* I can get help."
". . . *but* I'll get through it."
". . . *but* I don't have to do it perfectly."
". . . *but* I can just start and see how it goes."
". . . *but* it'll be really nice to have it out of the way."

Sometimes we need to persist in dealing with our internal "I can't" thinking, in order to prime the pump to launch that first step into action. Table 2.1 has some simple examples.

We often engage in basic everyday activities even when we don't want to (e.g., going to work, shopping, taking care of household chores, helping with children). Doing things such as this when we don't feel like it can increase our resilience over time. So jumping in with even bigger challenges can eventually begin to seem more natural. By helping others when we don't feel like it, we not only lighten their burden, but we also build stronger relationships with them. When we keep jumping in after we have not succeeded at something (think of Lincoln), we can develop determination in dealing with life's difficulties. All important endeavors begin with the first small step of jumping in.

Table 2.1 *But*-twists

Thought	*But*-twist
I can't do the dishes right now.	But it'll just take a few minutes.
I feel too lazy.	But it'll be nice to have them done.
Maybe my partner will do them.	But she'll really appreciate not having to do them.
This work project is too hard.	But I can start by writing down the steps I need to take to accomplish it.
I just can't do it.	But I can get help to figure it out.
It's hopeless.	But taking each little step one at a time is not hopeless. I'm merely feeling and thinking that it's hopeless.
I don't feel like studying.	But it won't kill me.
Watching TV sounds better.	But I can study for an hour and then go back to watching TV.
I just feel too lazy.	But I can get started now and relax again later.
I can't give this presentation.	But I can. It doesn't need to be perfect.
I feel too nervous.	But I can say the words, even if I simply read the whole thing.
It's just too hard.	But it won't kill me.

Tool #2. Activity Scheduling

A primary tool of behavioral activation is *activity scheduling*. In our complicated modern world, everyday living can seem overwhelming, which, in turn, can lead to inactivity. Maintaining a schedule or a simple, prioritized daily to-do list can help us remember and organize needful activities. Cognitive behavioral psychologists use a formal version of this process to help people who are experiencing depression activate behaviors that allow them to be more fully engaged in everyday living. With activity scheduling, daily tasks are broken down into small, easily accomplished actions. Included in this schedule are at least a few activities that are (1) easy enough to finish that day, and (2) personally enjoyable. This basic concept can have value for anyone desiring to increase satisfaction with their lives or simply wanting to get things done in a more effective and efficient manner.

In order to simplify our life and keep it going in the direction we really value, activity scheduling can take the form of daily action lists, such as the following.

- List key activities to be done that day. If they're difficult, try to break them down into smaller tasks.
- Prioritize a few weekly tasks that are important to your longer-term values and goals, not just tasks that are urgent.
- Include a few daily activities that are enjoyable.

Table 2.2 is a simple example of a basic daily action list. This type of list can be helpful for anyone, but it is particularly important if our inertia is keeping us from functioning or if we avoid completing valued activities in our lives.

When you create a schedule of activities, we suggest that you include a number of them. The more variety you have, the more likely your motivation to continue to activate behaviors will be, and the more balanced your life will become. Brainstorm a list of activities, including some that are inexpensive and free, and others that can be done all by yourself. You don't have to limit this list to activities you have done previously.

Table 2.2 Activity scheduling

	Week Beginning: __ / __ / ____		
DAY	**MORNING**	**AFTERNOON**	**EVENING**
Example	☐ Play with my dog ☐ Prepare and eat breakfast ☐ Go to work	☐ List my work tasks and begin the first one ☐ Eat my lunch outside	☐ Call a friend ☐ Stretch before taking a shower
Mon			
Tue			
Wed			
Thu			
Fri			
Sat			
Sun			

Note: Check off those planned activities that you actually did. You can write in any additional activity you may have done. You can also number each activity to indicate its priority.

Consider experimenting with new ones that are potentially satisfying and enjoyable.

As aids in structuring daily activities, you can use organizer software, a notebook, a simple calendar, or even post-its. Jumping in by proactively setting up appointments, meetings, and telephone or text communications can help force us to get things done. Until an activity is on the calendar, it may not happen.

The actor Drew Barrymore, who has suffered from depression through the years, described her very practical application of this activity scheduling principle: "I remind myself that when I'm daunted, just start, whether it's my mental wellness or stuff at work or cleaning the kitchen. Just start, don't stay stuck. Make the list, do that first thing on the list, and do whatever it takes to not sit and wallow in your crap."[6]

If avoiding certain behaviors has become particularly habitual and counterproductive, it may be beneficial to get help from clinicians trained in behavioral activation. They can provide structure through professional coaching, planning, problem solving, monitoring, and follow-up. Behavioral activation is considered to be part of the larger framework of cognitive behavioral therapy. Whereas CBT is sometimes more focused on changing unhelpful thoughts and beliefs, behavioral activation is primarily centered on changing actions (i.e., initiating helpful behaviors and stopping unhelpful ones). Some researchers have noted that behavioral activation might be as effective as CBT. It is also relatively uncomplicated, time efficient, and does not require complex skills from either patients or therapists.[7] Interest in and the use of behavioral activation has increased since the 1990s, inspired in part by the work of Neil Jacobsen and his colleagues.[8]

Tool #3. Living Our Values

Jumping in includes figuring out what we want to jump into. And the activities we jump into should logically be driven by what we most value. Each of us is a unique human being, and what we value is based on our specific personalities, interests, skills, and aspirations. We are born into a world that requires us to pursue some baseline activities, simply to function and survive. But we also quite naturally seek out meaning and enjoyment, based on what each of us values most.

Figuring out what we value gives clarity to our lives. It also provides us with a personal life compass, helping us not spend too much of our lives on activities that have little personal value. Depending on who we are, we might actually have a number of things that we value.

Kelly Wilson and colleagues have identified 10 domains to help people determine what they value.[9] They suggest reflecting on these values in two steps. First, rate the importance of each of these domains in our lives on a scale of 1 to 10, with 1 being extremely unimportant and 10 being extremely important. Second, use this prioritized list to assess the degree to which we are engaging in activities that are consistent with these values. Table 2.3 lists these value domains (to which we added an eleventh), with a column for recording its rating and two others for developing corresponding goals and desired activities.

As we determine our values, there are many questions we can ask ourselves. What do we truly care about? What do we really want to accomplish in life? What brings us satisfaction and enjoyment (i.e., happiness)? What are our natural interests, skills, and aspirations? What ethical principles are absolutely not negotiable for us? Wilson and his colleagues have suggested the following types of questions to help in determining our values.[10] First, what do you want your life to stand for? Second, what would you like to be remembered for? Phrased another way, in a world where you could choose to have your life be about something, what would you choose? It's never too late to examine and answer these kinds of questions.

Once we identify our prioritized values, they can be used to determine larger life goals that are consistent with those values.

- Be a good parent.
- Spend time with friends.

Table 2.3 Value domains

Domain	Importance (rate the value domain from 1, not important, to 10, very important)	Goals (what I ultimately want to accomplish in this domain)	Intentional activities (activities I can do to reach my goals for this domain)
1. *Family relations* What types of relationships do you want?			
2. *Marriage, couple relations* What type of partner do you want to be? What kind of relationship do you want?			
3. *Parenting* Do you want children? How do you want to raise your children? What sort of parent do you want to be?			
4. *Friendship, social life* What kind of social life do you want? What kind of friend do you want to be?			
5. *Career, employment* What are your income needs? What kind of work do you want to do? What path do you want to follow? What are the skills and experience you need?			
6. *Education, training, and personal growth* What are your needs and interests regarding education, cultural aspirations, and personal development?			

Domain	Importance (rate the value domain from 1, not important, to 10, very important)	Goals (what I ultimately want to accomplish in this domain)	Intentional activities (activities I can do to reach my goals for this domain)
7. *Recreation, fun* What do you like doing for enjoyment? What relaxes you? What feels like play? What hobbies, sports, and leisure activities do you like?			
8. *Spirituality* What spiritual and/or religious beliefs and practices do you value?			
9. *Citizenship, community life* What community, social, and activist causes, pursuits, and activities are important to you?			
10. *Health, physical well-being* What efforts do you value in terms of physical and mental health?			
11. *Ethics* [our addition] What rules of right and wrong are essential to you?			

- Help others.
- Protect the environment.
- Pursue a particular career path.
- Pursue a particular talent.
- Live a healthy lifestyle.
- Spend more time working for an important cause.
- Spend more time with an enjoyable hobby or the like.

These values and goals, however informal, can provide us with direction and commitment through the emotional ups and downs of life. Behavioral scientists maintain that having a broad array of valued interests can help us build up a stable and diverse set of activities and give robust meaning to our lives. If something happens that makes it impossible for us to continue in one domain (e.g., due to a physical impairment, a change of income or job, children growing up, a changed relationship), there are other activities and directions that can still provide enjoyment and satisfaction.

For the purposes of this book, we've added an eleventh domain, ethics—the rules of right and wrong that we commit to through thick and thin. Sometimes ethical standards can include too many rules, accompanied by too many unneeded judgments. But the core concept remains simple: some behaviors are better than others. (And, as we know only too well, some behaviors in history have been both tragic and horrific.) At a minimum, kindness is better than cruelty, honesty is better than dishonesty, and taking care of the Earth is better than destroying it. Core values about right and wrong are essential to both our our well-being and that of others. A very simple way of determining our ethical values is to consider how we would like to be treated. If we want to be treated with honesty, we value integrity. If we want to be treated fairly, we value justice. If we want to be treated with kindness, we value compassion. Of course the big ethical question is, Do we only care about whether we, our loved ones, and our "tribe" are treated in these ethical ways, or do we logically and compassionately want this for everyone and live our lives accordingly? (See box 2.1 for a suggestion on self-reflection by creating a *values and goals notebook*.)

Box 2.1

Values and Goals Notebook

Consider keeping a notebook, journal, or simple spreadsheet that lists your most important values, as well as the activities and projects you want to pursue in your life. This will provide you with overall clarity and direction, as well as affect the daily activities you choose to take on. This list doesn't need to be long or perfect, and it can be quite simple. What you value and choose to pursue will most likely change over time, but this list is a place to get started in confirming what you want to do with your life. Depending on how much structure you want, you can use this as a place to brainstorm the details of new projects you want to take on, following what it is that you value.

Sometimes we inherit values that we have not consciously chosen, but are given to us by our family, culture, or peers. We have lived with them for so long—perhaps since childhood—that they have become second nature to us. We might be living by rules and assumptions that we feel we should value, rather than what we really choose for ourselves. We may be involved in blind ambition, based on someone else's values, unless we actually stop and think about what we personally want. Notable people have taken this assertively independent path.

- Florence Nightingale, who lived at the same time as Abraham Lincoln, rejected the disapproval of her aristocratic British family and proactively chose her calling in nursing.
- The songwriter, performing artist, and Oxford University–educated Kris Kristofferson gave up a career as an officer in the US Army, along with the approval of his military father, in order to chart his own desired course.
- The mother of Isaac Newton wanted him to carry on the family tradition of farming, but after initially complying, he chose his own path and became one of the world's leading scientists.

Part of adult assertive living is to critically think about our beliefs and values and make sure they still work for us. Just because we're born into a specific belief system or culture, this by no means suggests that those beliefs or traditions are a good fit for our uniqueness. Maybe they are, but maybe not. Once again, our primary adult right is *to be the ultimate judge of what's best for us*.

Authentic values are not feelings; they are actions. We may not *feel* like living up to our values, but when it comes to truly authentic values, we do so anyway. As commentator Jon Stewart once put it, "If you don't stick to your values when they're being tested, they're not values—they're hobbies."[11]

Therefore, we take care of children, even when it's not enjoyable. We pursue our studies, even when we feel lazy. We take on a cause we believe in, even when it's a big challenge. We tell the truth, even when we are afraid.

Spending too much time on things we don't value can become a life half lived. *Living up to our values* means doing more of the things that are truly important to us and less of those we don't value—that is, letting go of unproductive activities that can lead us far astray. To help us in this process, we can think about the following:

- Consider our daily activities and how much time we spend on those we don't value or that don't at least support the things we value.
- Consider any big moves we need to make to more fully live our values (new careers, a bigger commitment to particular interests or causes, re-energized relationships).
- If big moves are not practically doable for the time being, consider smaller ways (*pockets of time*) to insert what we value into our daily lives.

Finding Pockets of Time for What We Value

Only a few rare and lucky people can turn their passion into a full-time career and earn sufficient income from it. This doesn't mean that we have to give up on something we highly value. Instead, we can find pockets of time for them. We don't need to pursue our passions as a full-time source of income. We can also live them for free.

Cynthia Kersey's book *Unstoppable* includes the story of Canadian business executive Robyn Allan. At the age of 16, Allan had taken her first dance class and fell in love with the notion of becoming a dancer. Her parents had also taught her an old adage: "If you can't be excellent at something, don't do it." Since she had a passion for dance but was never going to be an extraordinarily talented dancer, she let go of her dream and continued on with her life, pursuing a successful career in business and raising a family. But her passion for dance—a very important personal value—never completely went away. When she was in her thirties, rather than working late once again, she jumped in a cab one day and returned to her dance lessons. She rearranged her life to make time for work, family, and dance—even having her children participate in her dance-related activities. Eventually she would produce, choreograph, and perform in dance productions for large audiences in Canada. She would also go on to become the chief executive officer of the Insurance Corporation of British Columbia in Canada. By reconfirming what she valued and making a commitment to those values, she was able to find room for an activity that formed a very meaningful part of her life. Allan once wrote, "Many of us are afraid to follow our passions, to pursue what we want most because it means taking risks and even facing failure. But to pursue your passion with all your heart and soul is success in itself."[12]

Behavioralists make the obvious point that part of fostering life satisfaction is simply *doing more of the things we enjoy and less of the things we don't*. Pragmatically, in a world of competing needs and interests, this isn't always possible. Depending on what our long-term values and goals are, we may need to engage in a lot of short-term activities that we don't enjoy at all. Our full-time vocation may not provide full-time bliss. But we can still carve out pockets of time for the things we value most, whether those pockets mean spending time with family and friends or participating in music, sports, art, outdoor activities, public service, faith communities, exercise, learning, travel, dance, or wherever else our values and interests take us. At least a few of our daily to-do items should be fun and invigorating, however brief.

Scott is innately an outdoors and nature-oriented person. But as life would have it, he has spent most of his professional career indoors—quite often, behind a desk. He quickly discovered that within his work life, he really needed to add pockets of time spent in the outdoors and nature to his daily experience. Early on, he gained an identity as the guy not to be found during his "lunchtime constitutional." His working colleagues learned to accept this. His daily outdoor walks became sacred, and they provided just enough of a pocket of time to foster greater enjoyment in his everyday life. John Muir, the famous naturalist, maintained a day job, first as a machinist and then as a farmer/businessman, but he always carved out abundant time for both ventures into the natural world and his assertive activism on behalf of nature.

If we are fortunate enough to have sufficient material goods to meet our needs, we need to take care that these pockets of time don't entirely vanish in a constant pursuit of more of those goods. Prominent happiness researcher Ed Diener, maintains that happiness is *"psychological* wealth." While a certain level of financial security is important to reduce worry and increase our well-being, studies show that additional financial wealth does little to further add to our happiness.[13] Diener is convinced that much of our happiness is connected with *doing*, rather than *having*. It's more about the daily journey than the place of arrival. It's more about driving a car along a beautiful coastline than owning the latest-model automobile. This remains true, whether that *doing* is going to work, pursuing a valued goal, helping others, looking out for our physical health, participating in a fun activity, enjoying the company of others, engaging in meditation, reading a book, or relaxing on a beach. Activating behavior isn't just about physical behavior, it's about intentionally taking part in any valued or needful mental or physical activity.

Depending on our stage in life and the amount of free time we have available, we also may find it valuable to create a master list of activities, reminding us of the options that bring us the most satisfaction and enjoyment. (Maybe this list can become part of your values and goals notebook.) And if we are in a more depressed frame of mind, where it's difficult for us to either think or become active, this type of list might provide some immediate guidance. There are many examples of activities lists and menus on the internet. Go to a search engine and simply type in "activity lists for behavioral activation." The results will provide sets of ideas, from which you can customize your own.

SUMMARY OF TOOLS IN THIS CHAPTER

But-**twists**: using a "but" rebuttal to "I can't" thinking.
Activity scheduling: using schedules, action lists, or calendars to plan daily activities.
Living our values: confirming what we value, and pursuing our life goals and activities accordingly.

CHAPTER 3

Embracing Compassion
Emotional Assertiveness

The biggest challenge to our emotional lives is suffering. We equate emotional assertiveness with compassion, which is defined as *intentionally responding to suffering through helpful words and actions*. This applies to both the suffering of others and our own.

Human suffering is the sensation we feel when experiencing physical or emotional pain. Suffering can take the form of agony, distress, worry, fear, anxiety, depression, and grief. It can be driven by physical ailments, hunger, poverty, and difficult life events, as well as by our own innate mental and emotional traits and conditions. Regardless of its initial cause, suffering always has a major emotional component.

Anyone who has spent time around a group of small children quickly comes to realize that suffering is an innate part of human life. Children can be fed, well rested, and free from physical needs, yet they can still collapse into torrents of tears. From childhood on, it's very clear that suffering is not an abnormality but rather is a natural, built-in *part* of human life.

Our thinking and our emotions are bound together with multiple connections, based on nature, nurture, and cultural conditioning. Negative emotions are triggered not just by real threats and problems but also by our mind's sophisticated ability to imagine, remember the past, and forecast the future. Almost any thought or memory can trigger a painful emotion. Just the memories of a loved one who is no longer with us can bring on sorrow; fearing a potential job loss can create intense worry; ruminating over past mistakes or rejections can trigger anxiety. Our minds instinctively scan our personal worlds on an ongoing basis, on the lookout for threats—real and imagined—involving the past, present, and future. We feel the worry and fear that such thoughts engender. Suffering is the price we pay for being human.

OUR SHARED HUMANITY

Compassion starts with acknowledging the reality of our shared human condition—seeing people in our everyday lives as other selves, instead of viewing them simply as objects. Recognizing them as ends in and of themselves, not merely as means. Life is filled with adverse situations, and we can never fully know what difficulties other people are dealing with, be they mental, emotional, or physical. Yet even if we cannot always know what they are going through, we can still treat them as other "selves" who may need our concern and help. As the Dalai Lama stated, "Love and compassion are necessities, not luxuries. Without them humanity cannot survive."[1]

Helping Is Basic to Human Experience

While it's true that we're born with a strong self-interest (i.e., survival) instinct, it's also true that we're born with an instinct and abilities to help. A variety of studies on infants have revealed that children as young as 14 to 18 months old exhibit helping behaviors, even if they are given no external rewards for these actions. Very young children naturally engage in helping, sharing, and comforting. They try to voluntarily assist with housework and chores almost as soon as they can move around. They show distress at another's suffering and are relieved when seeing that suffering alleviated. And *prosocial behavior*—intended to help or benefit another person or group—generally continues to increase across preschool and childhood.[2] Other studies suggest that in older children and adults, when given an opportunity to benefit others, often their first and most automatic impulse is to do so.[3]

It's also clear that helping is good for us. A long-term, ongoing study in Germany regarding life satisfaction (the largest of its kind) shows that people have achieved long-term increases in life satisfaction by engaging in goals and activities relating to altruism (friendships, helping others, activism). Studies in the United Kingdom and Australia have shown similar outcomes.[4] There is also a developing area of research suggesting that helping—in the forms of providing social support, being a caregiver for an ill family member, and volunteering—is frequently associated with better physical and mental health outcomes for the helper.[5] We were meant to help and to be helped.

FOUR TOOLS FOR BUILDING MORE COMPASSION INTO OUR LIVES

We don't have to love people, or even like them, to have compassion for them. Compassion is not wanting people to suffer, whether we like them or not. It means assertively responding to human suffering with words and actions demonstrating concern and help. Compassion doesn't always come easily.

This is why it is often an assertive choice and an intentional activity. To one degree or another, we're all born with an innate ability to help, share, and comfort, but sometimes we need to consciously activate it. The following are four tools to cultivate more compassion in our lives.

Tool #1. Rational Compassion

In academic research, *compassion* is defined as concern for human suffering, combined with a desire to help alleviate that suffering.[6] There is both an affective (emotional) component and a cognitive (thinking) component to having concern for others. *Empathy* is the emotional ability to feel what others are feeling, and *sympathy* is the ability to feel sorrow for others in their suffering. Both traits can help drive and sustain compassion. As with any human trait, however, some people have more natural empathy and sympathy, and others have less. The former instinctively jump in, expressing concern and a desire to help, while the latter seem to lack this natural feeling for others.

What do we do if, based on our unique emotional thermostat, we simply don't feel as much empathy or compassion for others? Or perhaps our cultural experience has desensitized us to the plights of others. Paul Bloom, a professor of psychology, makes a case for what he calls *rational compassion*: compassion based on reason, rather than pure emotion.[7] He isn't necessarily talking about this as a panacea for empathy-deficient people, but as a broader consideration. He takes the position that compassion can be problematic if our desire to help others is based purely on emotion, without also thinking through what's the best way to help someone in a given situation or seeing whether help is even warranted. He points out that it's the ability of doctors, nurses, psychologists, and first responders to set aside their emotions in a particular moment that allows them to effectively and rationally deal with life-threatening emergencies, as well as human suffering in general. Empathy may be a good general motivator when it comes to compassion, but it can also be compassionate to think rationally about choosing when and how to help. Rational compassion provides a path for helping others, both for people who have ample emotional empathy and those who have little.

When it comes to helping, rational compassion means not always acting via the emotion of compassion (or lack thereof), but thinking things through. It can include the following kinds of considerations (similar to the kinds of questions a hospital nurse might ask).

- Is this urgent?
- How can I be most effective, given my resources?
- What response is in the best long-term interest of this person?
- If I'm thinking of making a bigger commitment, what are my priorities, and how do I get the biggest bang for my time or financial involvement (i.e., what are the costs and benefits)?
- How can I make sure that this request for help is legitimate? Are dishonesty or manipulation in play here?

If we are on the low end of the natural emotional compassion scale, another way to engage in rational compassion is through *perspective taking* (i.e., thinking through another's point of view). When in doubt, we can follow the golden rule: "How would I like to be treated in this situation?" Research shows that training in role-playing (i.e., direct perspective taking), results in increased thoughts and feelings of compassion.

In a review of research on empathy and social functioning, Mark H. Davis concluded that perspective taking was the aspect of empathy that had the most impact, actually making a difference in social relationships.[8]

Chuck Feeney is an extraordinary example of both placing value on social well-being and having rational compassion. Feeney grew up in New Jersey during the Great Depression, served in the US Air Force right after World War II, and ended up having a knack for business. He ultimately developed a very successful company, focused on duty-free shopping. He plowed his profits into land, hotels, retail stores, clothing companies, and (later) high-tech startups. By the age of 50, he had amassed an immense fortune, along with all the properties and luxury goods such a fortune can buy.

Nonetheless, he ultimately discovered that he was living a life that was disconnected from his highest personal values. He spent the next several years giving away almost all of his wealth—$8.6 billion—to initiatives meant to help other people around the world. This included large contributions to education, medical research and health care, science, and the peace process in Northern Ireland, among other significant endeavors. By the end of his life, he had a very modest lifestyle, living in a small, two-bedroom rental apartment in San Francisco. In the process of helping others, he applied rational compassion—using a rigorous process to determine how he could get the biggest impact from his contributions. He cared about priorities, results, and not wasting resources.[9] His contributions were anonymous, and he often required that the funds be matched, in order to encourage others to also participate and get even more benefit from his investment. His work influenced Warren Buffett and Bill Gates when they launched the Giving Pledge in 2010—an effort to have the wealthiest people in the world make a commitment to give away at least half of their fortunes to charitable causes.[10]

We live in a world of much human need, and at times it seems like anything we do will be just a drop in the bucket, especially if we compare ourselves with the Chuck Feeneys of the world—people with enormous financial means and extremely generous hearts. But, however small the amount, it's never a drop in the bucket for the specific individuals we help. If it is our own children, parents, or other family members receiving help, we would not see it as a drop in the bucket. And so it is with any other needful person or cause. The icon of full-measured compassion, Mother Teresa, once wrote, "Every work of love is a work of peace, no matter how small it is."[11] She also stated, "The fruit of love is service, which is compassion in action."[12]

Tool #2. Jumping In and Helping

The tools for behavioral activation discussed in chapter 2 have a direct application when it comes to helping others. Just as action sometimes precedes motivation, compassionate action sometimes precedes the emotion of compassion. Rather than waiting for a compassionate emotion to motivate us to help others, we can take a leap of faith. If others really need our help, we *jump in and help* them, even when we don't feel like it. When there are chores to be done around the house, rather than assuming someone else will take care of them, we can jump in and do them. If there are important things that need to be done to help our friends, neighbors, coworkers, or community, we can jump in and share our skills and energy with them. Our bodies—if healthy—were meant to be active, and we can accomplish much on behalf of others simply by jumping in and doing.

In Scott's personal life, his mother-in-law provided a stellar example of compassionate jumping in to help someone. For Willy, as she was commonly known, nursing was a calling, not just a profession. Whether at a hospital, nursing home, or veterans' home, she took direct ownership of each patient's physical and emotional care. While she certainly had natural empathy and sympathy, the main focus of her compassion was listening and helping. She took a genuine interest in everyone she came in contact with, whether at work, in her home, or in her community. She would know more about a person's life in 10 minutes than many of us would know in a year. She was also unusually nimble in transitioning from listening and talking to helping, just as soon as she saw a need. She was most at home offering food, cleaning up, or running an errand for someone. She exemplified the premise that jumping in and helping is often the most assertively compassionate thing we can do. This may be especially true if we have less natural empathy and sympathy. We can still see a need, apply perspective taking, and jump in to help, even if it's only to just be there.

The Irish musician Bono (Paul David Hewson) and his wife Alison are iconic examples of jumping in to help, even with full personal lives. It's clear from his autobiography, *Surrender*, that Bono hasn't always had all the answers when he first jumps into entrenched problems of poverty. But as an antipoverty campaigner, he has artfully used his fame to jump in, get himself up to speed on the details of solutions, and figure out a way to get results. In the process, he has made an enormous difference in helping others across the globe: getting funding, food, and medications to people who need them. He writes, "What works? That's what I'm always asking. When whoever said the job of the artist it to describe the problem, not solve it, I wasn't paying attention. I want to be with the people who follow through and actually make things actually better."[13]

In the thirteenth century CE, Dōgen Zenji, the founder of the Soto school of Zen in Japan, gave this simple advice to his students regarding assertive compassion: "Just practice good, do good for others, without thinking of making yourself known so that you may gain reward. Really bring benefit to others, gaining nothing for yourself. This is the primary requisite for breaking free of attachments to the self."[14]

Tool #3. Positive Communication

One of the most compassionate things we can do, on a mundane everyday basis, is to communicate with others in an inclusive, positive manner. Happiness researcher Barbara Fredrickson has suggested that a 3:1 ratio of positivity to negativity is a tipping point in terms of human well-being and performance (even if it's only a mild form of positivity). At that point—and beyond—people are more likely to flourish.[15] The communications we make and receive each day can impact that ratio. (One reason why too much media/news exposure is not altogether healthy is that bad news negatively impacts emotions.) Rejection from others produces a painful reaction that is virtually the same as physical pain.[16] We are emotionally wired to suffer if we are treated poorly by others.

In our own modest way, we can promote well-being and alleviate suffering on a daily basis through our gift of inclusive, *positive communication*, based not only on what we tell others, but also on what we tell ourselves. We can provide

- compliments,
- encouragement,
- gratitude,

- sympathy,
- comfort,
- positive suggestions, and
- constructive critical input (without the guilt).

This type of intentional compassion costs us nothing, but it has the potential to lift others. Researcher John Gottman has found that healthy marriages generally require five positive communications to offset each negative communication.[17] Marcial Losada and Emily Heaphy have studied the characteristics of highly successful business teams and found that the highest-performing teams had a 6:1 ratio between positive and negative communications among themselves, while the lowest-performing teams had a 1:1 ratio.[18] Clearly, positive communications are quite important to social well-being. And, if we can't readily alleviate suffering through our communication style, can we at least not add to it?

The speaking-up skills described in chapter 1, which are helpful in dealing with shyness, are also quite useful for engaging in the compassion of positive communication. Speaking up with kindness to express sincere compliments and gratitude fosters goodwill and positive emotions. Naoki, in some of his work with assertiveness, suggests that we take the time to be specific with our compliments and gratitude, so people are aware that we've noticed and believe that our communications are authentic.

We can also provide positive communication in ways that are deep and profound. We might be the one pivotal voice of compassion for someone who doesn't receive this anywhere else. In *Soul Models*, Mary Griffith shares an extremely difficult but important part of her life story. She had been raised in a very restrictive religious household, where beliefs were to be accepted and not questioned. One of the beliefs she had been taught was that being gay was a "sin." She carried this certainty into adulthood and then motherhood. As a result, she was mortified when she discovered that her second son, Bobby, was gay. She could not accept this reality and actively worked to get him to change. Based on how she was raised, she thought she was doing what was best for her son. But it wasn't, and her life was shattered the day that Bobby committed suicide.

Her deep grief motivated her to learn more. She concluded that acceptance of and compassion for her son should always have been her total focus. She subsequently became an activist, speaking out, wherever she could, to parents and young people. She recounted her story and emphasized the need for all parents to accept and love their children unconditionally—including communicating understanding and compassion to them. She stated, "The number one message I want to share with parents is to listen to your children. . . . Put aside your own feelings and hear what they are saying, whatever it is—love does not draw a line in the sand."[19]

Tool #4. Compassion-Based Meditations

A very specific tool for cultivating compassionate feelings and attitudes consists of *compassion-based meditations*. Jumping in and helping develops compassion from the outside in, while meditation does so from the inside out. Current research on the outcomes of meditation-based approaches to developing compassion suggests that meditation enhances compassion on both an emotional and a behavioral basis.[20] These outcomes seem to be triggered not only by compassion-based meditation, but also by mindfulness meditation more generally (discussed in chapter 4).

Two forms of compassion-based meditation, originally coming out of Buddhist tradition, are loving-kindness meditation and compassion meditation. Loving-kindness meditation focuses on holding ourselves and others in our hearts and minds with loving kindness. Compassion meditation is similar, although it is focused specifically on those we have reason to believe are suffering.

Loving-kindness meditation

Practitioners of *loving-kindness meditation* suggest that we take time each day to become still and consciously invite words and feelings of kindness, compassion, and a warm acceptance of the people in our lives, including ourselves. They suggest holding others in our mind's eye, wishing them freedom from suffering, wishing them happiness, and cherishing them. When we bestow blessings and peace upon people, it is more difficult to hold on to animosity.

Loving-kindness meditation typically begins with ourselves, first basking in our own kindness and wishing ourselves well, and then expanding this attitude to others: loved ones, our community, humanity, and, ultimately, difficult people with whom we are not on good terms. But the order in which we include individuals in this expansion, and the words we use, can take any form, as long as it helps us soften our attitude towards people and their suffering.

By searching online, you can find abundant information on the details of loving-kindness meditation. The elements of this type of meditation are generally described as follows.

1. For a few minutes, stabilize and calm the mind by focusing awareness on our breath.

2. Invoke feelings of loving kindness toward ourselves by saying things like "May I be free from suffering," "May I be at peace," and "May I be happy." These are traditional phrases for loving-kindness meditation, but they may feel too lofty or unrealistic for your tastes. If so, consider "May things be OK," May I have greater peace," and "May I accept myself with compassion."
3. Next, expand these same feelings toward our loved ones, as we visualize them and hold them in our hearts with love (in this case, applying the second type of examples of phrasing mentioned above): "May they be OK," "May they have greater peace," and "May they receive compassion." This can include family members and friends. For the moment, we completely forget about whatever may be their faults or their shortcomings and focus only on our love and best wishes for them.
4. Expand these feelings to neighbors, coworkers, and others.
5. Expand these feelings to people we may have a more difficult time with, perhaps someone we don't really like or have much sympathy for—the more difficult acquaintances in our life.
6. Expand these feelings to all people who are suffering, to victims of injustice, and to those in need of care and compassion.

Compassion meditation

While loving-kindness meditation focuses on generating feelings of loving-kindness for people in general, *compassion meditation* targets people whom we have reason to believe are going through significant suffering. Formal compassion meditation involves (1) envisioning the suffering of a specific person or group of people; (2) applying mindful attention to our sensations, thoughts, and feelings that arise as we envision this suffering; and (3) cultivating thoughts and feelings of care, concern, and a desire to relieve suffering.[21]

The Buddhist teacher and writer Jack Kornfield provides these simple phrases for less formal compassion meditation, first picturing specific people in our minds, and then expanding this, more abstractly, to others in our community and world who are suffering.[22]

> "May you be held in compassion."
> "May your pain and sorrow be eased."
> "May you be at peace."

Next, apply this to yourself.

> "May I be held in compassion."
> "May my pain and sorrow be eased."
> "May I be at peace."

If we're not into meditation, we might consider using the above phrases in our everyday lives as simple mental well wishing, especially when we experience unneeded negative thoughts and feelings about other people. If we are people of religious faith, we might use these kinds of words as brief prayer phrases for those we know are suffering.

> "Bless _____ with comfort and strength."
> "Bless _____, so their pain and sorrow might be eased."
> "Bless _____, so they might be at peace."

SELF-COMPASSION

With *self-compassion*, we don't need emotional empathy or sympathy to try to understand our suffering—we're experiencing our suffering directly and know what it feels like only too well. What we really need is our own compassionate help and comfort. We need to stop judging and criticizing ourselves, and instead we can embrace ourselves with kindness. Self-compassion is applying the golden rule in the opposite direction: treating ourselves as we would treat our best friends or close family members. Much of this begins with unconditional self-acceptance through thick and thin. For our wellbeing, we can be at least as kind to ourselves as we are to our loved ones. We can have concern for ourselves, and speak to ourselves, as we would to a good friend.

Kristen Neff, in *Self-Compassion*, has identified the following three core components for helping to cultivate self-compassion.[23]

1. *Self-kindness* involves giving ourselves the same kindness, care, and comfort we would give to a treasured loved one. We offer ourselves warmth and understanding when we are suffering, make mistakes, or go through difficult times. This can take the form of physical kindness (taking the time to do activities that are enjoyable and soothing to us) and mental/verbal kindness (giving ourselves words of comfort, sympathy, forgiveness, and understanding, thus allowing perspective taking and unconditional acceptance).
2. *Common humanity* is the human condition in which we all share. Self-compassion is benefited by reminding ourselves that being human is not easy. We are imperfect,

just like everyone else. It is easy to believe that we are the only one who makes mistakes and experiences misfortune. But just look around. Recognizing our shared humanity with others—reminding ourselves that pain, imperfections, and difficulties are a regular part of life for all of us—can help us develop greater skill in perspective taking.

3. *Mindfulness* is paying attention to our experiences with nonjudgmental awareness. In the case of self-compassion, this means paying particular attention to our feelings of suffering, approaching them without judgment and with tenderness and understanding. It means not taking these emotions too personally, as if they were "us." This suffering occurs as an aspect of our bodies and the human condition in general. But experiencing these emotions does not lessen us in any possible way. This kind of mindfulness includes holding difficult thoughts and feelings in nonjudgmental awareness (not trying to avoid or get rid of them) while maintaining unconditional acceptance and love for ourselves in the process.

Self-compassion means letting go of the burden of being too critical, harsh, and judgmental about ourselves. In part, this comes about by fully accepting that we're human. Until we do so, we will be bogged down by self—feeling pressure to overly protect ourselves, seeking approval from others, and focusing too much energy and time on our emotional lives. Being kind to ourselves, and less judgmental, frees us up emotionally, so we have more time and energy for others. According to research in the field of self-compassion, self-compassion efforts have been found to increase optimism and life satisfaction, and to decrease depression and negative body judgments.[24]

THE COMPASSION OF HEROISM

Given that there remains an abundance of evil in the world (i.e., cruelty in all its ugly and sometimes violent forms), and that evil can be dangerous, sometimes compassion must take on the much more assertive/aggressive form of *heroism*. Heroism is taking compassionate action in the face of personal risk and sacrifice. The world requires heroism, in order to protect the innocent, stop evil, and stand up for justice. There are too many examples throughout history of well-meaning people unintentionally contributing to suffering in the world by not urgently and assertively resisting cruel and abusive human activity. "The only thing necessary for the triumph of evil is for good people to do nothing" continues to ring loud and clear.[25] Heroes recognize the suffering of victims to the point of being moved to action to protect them and fight back. Assertively defending and protecting the innocent is as compassionate—and sometimes even more important and urgent—than peaceful acts of kindness. There are heroes across the globe—including many honorable people in the military and law enforcement—who have even been willing to give up their own lives in order to protect the innocent.

Probably no public figure exemplified greater heroism and resistance to cruelty and injustice than Rolihlahla (Nelson) Mandela. Mandela's father was the principal counselor to the acting king of the Thembu, but he died when Nelson was just 12 years old. Mandela and a colleague established South Africa's first Black law firm. During his lifetime, he and his fellow native South Africans were not allowed the basic freedoms of movement, speech, the right to vote, or self-determination. They were forced to live in isolated degradation and poverty. Mandela initially sought freedom through nonviolent political means, but when the government refused to provide basic rights to the country's Black majority—and enforced that refusal with violence—Mandela supported armed resistance. Because of this, when he was 45 years old, he was put into prison for 27 years. He could have left prison on three different occasions if he would have abandoned his support for the resistance efforts, but he declined each time. He patiently lived with the degradations of prison life, spending much of the time working in a limestone quarry and eventually contracting tuberculosis. When he was freed from prison at age 72, instead of indulging in his anger, he let go of it and compassionately worked toward building a unified nation. Mandela once wrote, "Our human compassion binds us the one to the other—not in pity or patronizingly, but as human beings who have learned how to turn our common suffering into hope for the future."[26]

A note on moral elevation. These acts of heroic compassion also help society through *moral elevation*. When observing or hearing about an exemplary act of compassion, people commonly feel the natural, awe-related emotion of moral elevation. While we are particularly inspired by acts of heroism, we are also inspired by everyday acts of compassion. Self-reporting measures confirm that after experiencing moral elevation, people feel more optimistic about humanity and are motivated to help others.[27] We have an instinct to help, and we are inspired by the compassion of others. We are not only affected by our personal DNA, but we are also heavily influenced by the cultures we live in. By our own examples, we can assertively contribute to cultures of compassion.

SUMMARY OF TOOLS IN THIS CHAPTER

Rational compassion: applying reason to compassion, whether or not we *feel* compassion.
Jumping in to help: actively assisting others, even when we don't feel like it.
Positive communication: helping others through kind and supportive words.
Compassion-based meditations: applying meditation to foster a more compassionate attitude.

CHAPTER 4

Accepting Life

Mental Assertiveness

We define *mental assertiveness* as fostering greater acceptance of life by *intentionally reducing unneeded negative judgment*. Too many negative evaluations, including of ourselves and other people, leads to dissatisfaction with life and negative emotions—the two factors that define human unhappiness.

We humans were meant to *experience life*: to experience thoughts, emotions, physicality, choices, efforts, relationships, love, and the joys and challenges of this beautiful but difficult physical world. We can accept this experience or not, but here we are, nonetheless.

Dutch author J. J. van der Leeuw put it most succinctly when he wrote, "The mystery of life is not a problem to be solved; it is a reality to be experienced."[1] Eleanor Roosevelt expanded on this basic point: "The purpose of life after all is to live it, to taste experience to the utmost, to reach out eagerly and without fear for newer and richer experience."[2]

THE PURPOSE OF LIFE IS TO EXPERIENCE LIFE

As we all know, life is a journey with a full spectrum of pleasures and pains.

- Sunshine and storm.
- Health and illness.
- Abundance and scarcity.
- Joy and grief.
- Solutions and problems.
- Fun and boredom.
- Ease and difficulty.
- Love and cruelty.
- Peace and conflict.
- Birth and death.

Few people have experienced the full gamut of life as dramatically as actor Michael J. Fox. Growing up in a family of modest means in Canada, Fox had natural artistic talent—not just for acting, but also for music, drawing, and writing. He participated in all of his school's theatrical productions and loved hockey. His first break came when he was 15 and was hired as part of the cast for the Canadian Broadcast Corporation's sitcom *Leo and Me*. He eventually moved to Hollywood to seek his fortune, living on a shoestring budget until he landed his life-changing role as Alex Keaton in the sitcom *Family Ties*. He was just 21, and his professional and financial life changed overnight. He eventually starred in the *Back to the Future* franchise and had other notable movie and TV roles. By the age of 25, he had achieved the heights of professional and financial success.

But, as is also well known, at the age of 29 he was diagnosed with a rare form of young-onset Parkinson's disease. As Fox documents in *Lucky Man*,[3] he was in denial about the disease for quite some time. As part of this denial, he went into a downward spiral of alcohol abuse and depression. A big part of his eventual rebound was *accepting* this new development in his life and adjusting accordingly, rather than continuing to fight reality. He stopped drinking, got professional therapy, and forged ahead in new ways. He not only made modifications to his acting career and personal life, but he also reconfirmed his most essential values and priorities and began to live them in deeper ways, particularly his commitment to his family. He became a leading spokesperson and advocate for Parkinson's research.

During his rebound, nearly every day Fox would say the serenity prayer: "God, grant me the serenity to accept the things I cannot change, courage to change the things I can, and wisdom to know the difference." Regarding the impact of acceptance in his life, he once said, "My happiness goes in proportion to my acceptance, and in inverse proportion to my expectations. The more I expect, the more unhappy I am going to be. The more I accept, the more serene I am."[4] Following surgery for a spinal tumor in 2018 (unrelated to his Parkinson's), which left him needing to relearn how to walk in the midst of his underlying disease, he said, "You can be a realist and an optimist at the same time. If I don't accept it, I can't move forward."[5]

Acceptance is seeing life for what it is, without denial and without the expectation that it needs to be something different when it can't be, including the many things that are outside of our choices and our control. Acceptance of life is the degree to which we're willing to accept reality with more understanding and perspective, and fewer negative judgments—that is, with less turmoil and more willingness and compassion.

CHOOSING GREATER ACCEPTANCE

There are clear benefits to developing *greater acceptance* in our lives by reducing our negative judgments. Over the past few decades, cognitive- and acceptance-based practices—focused on reducing negative judgments—have demonstrated clinical effectiveness in helping people deal with anxiety-related symptoms.[6] Research on the elderly suggests that the emotional well-being of older adults can actually increase, due to their greater acceptance of both life experiences and the unpleasant emotions that sometimes accompany them.[7] Studies have consistently demonstrated that self-acceptance reduces anxiety and fosters a greater acceptance of others.[8] Greater acceptance of life leads to less dissatisfaction, which results in having fewer of the negative emotions that come with dissatisfaction.

The challenge in acceptance is that we instinctively judge the difficult parts of life negatively. We're structured this way for physical survival, when quick negative judgments can make the difference between life and death. Asking ourselves not to judge is like asking ourselves not to breathe. Scientists tell us that we're also born with a "negativity bias." Negativity is meant to be a strong sensation that gets our attention. So not only do we have an instinct for making judgments, but we are also drawn to paying close attention to the negative. For everyday living, this natural tendency toward negative judgment works against acceptance. Our bodies (and our emotions) are primarily built for survival, not for bliss. The challenge is that, given our capacity to remember, imagine, and forecast, we can experience these negative sensations much more often—and more strongly—than we need to.

Despite this natural tendency toward negativity, we, as adults, also have the ability to strive for greater acceptance. Acceptance is an intentional mental activity. It requires us to slow down, get a different perspective, and reduce our negative judgments. It means learning to observe life more and evaluate it less. We can wish that we would not make mistakes, that all of our choices would be successful, that other people would always be kind, and that tragedy would not happen in the world—but this is not the world we live in. Continuing to ruminate over life's difficulties and assessing them negatively does us no good.

Another actor, the Dutch British actress Audrey Hepburn, had her life turned upside down as a young girl. Her father left the family when she was just 6 years old, and she was 10 when Nazi Germany invaded the Netherlands. She, her mother, stepbrothers, grandparents, uncle, and aunt were forced to suffer the deprivations and violence of this occupation. Her uncle was executed by German soldiers. Toward the end of World War II, her city became a major battleground between Allied and German forces, resulting in tragic devastations for civilians. For months she lived without having light, heat, or adequate water, and with very little food—sometimes going for days without anything to eat. She learned quite young about the full spectrum of potential life circumstances. She once said, "I decided very early on, just to accept life unconditionally. I never expected it to do anything special for me, yet I seemed to accomplish far more than I had ever hoped."[9] Her life circumstances changed dramatically following the war. In addition to a very successful acting career (including an Academy Award for best actress at age 25), later in life she became a humanitarian ambassador for UNICEF, an agency of the United Nations seeking relief for impoverished children across the globe. She was never in denial about the devastations of her young life. She accepted them and used them as powerful motivators for doing good in the world.

ACCEPTANCE IS NOT RESIGNATION

To be clear, acceptance is not resignation. Acceptance doesn't mean that we have to like events in our lives or judge them positively. It means that, instead of mentally battling with and denying the world and its myriad details, causing ourselves further emotional upheaval, we acknowledge difficulties as part of life.

We define *acceptance* as intentionally reducing unneeded negative judgments. But there is still a critical role and purpose for *needed* negative judgments and the emotions that come with them. This not only applies to quick negative assessments for personal survival and to everyday problem solving, but also to helping others and to the ethical judgments necessary for responding to injustices in the world. We can accept the nature and reality of life while also clearly seeing the negative consequences of disease, poverty, and life's other painful challenges. Acceptance doesn't mean that we stop doing everything in our power to make the world a better place for ourselves and others. As exemplified by Michael J. Fox and Audrey Hepburn, accepting the realities of life can help us see life more clearly and honestly—with less denial—and motivates us to assert ourselves in new and important ways.

FOUR TOOLS FOR DEVELOPING GREATER ACCEPTANCE

Greater acceptance requires perspective taking and reducing unneeded negative judgments, both of which can be supported by the following:

1. Remembering "big idea" perspectives.
2. Disputing exaggerated negative thinking.
3. Maintaining core beliefs that promote acceptance.
4. Practicing and applying principles of nonjudgmental awareness (mindfulness).

Tool #1. Remembering "Big Idea" Perspectives

One of the core ideas behind cognitive behavioral psychology is that our perceptions and thinking can impact our emotions. If we think negatively about the weather, the economy, our neighbors, our coworkers, our work, and the like, we automatically feel greater stress, irritation, and worry. If we dwell on past mistakes, we're bound to feel more anxious or depressed. If we ruminate about what can go wrong in the future, we'll feel more worried. But if we soften our negative judgments and have greater acceptance of the ebb and flow of life, we feel fewer negative emotions.

It's also the case that our minds like simplicity. This can work against us when we apply simplistic negative labels to people and events, such as bad, horrible, terrible, stupid, and the like. But it can work in our favor when we remember big, simple, core truths that can help us gain perspective through the ups and downs of life. In the case of acceptance, these ideas focus on softening our natural tendency towards negative judgments. Here are three self-evident, big-picture truths that can help us gain perspective in times of difficulty.

"It's part of life"
If we could commit ourselves to just one core idea in support of acceptance, it would be the simple but powerful concept that difficulty is a regular *part of life*. The advantage of reminding ourselves of this very basic truth in times of difficulty and frustration is that we need not assess an event as being either positive or negative, but simply acknowledge its reality, with less emotional turmoil. The point is to have a go-to phrase that we can tell ourselves in response to difficult events, helping us get a broader perspective and reducing negative emotions.

A similar powerful phrase is "It is what it is." The essence of acceptance is an ability to see and understand reality without always having to evaluate it. If you find that negative judgments are making your life less satisfying and enjoyable, consider the following types of phrases.

- "It's part of life."
- "That's life."
- "It is what it is."
- "That's how it goes."
- "This cold weather is just part of life."
- "Mistakes are part of life. I'll learn from them and move on."
- "I don't like it, but irritating (arrogant, combative, mean, greedy) people are part of life."
- "That wasn't such a great decision, but not being able to predict the future is part of life."
- "Getting sick is no fun, but it's part of life."
- "I hate this traffic, but it's just part of life."

The use of this big idea perspective was exemplified by Zeno, the founder of the Stoic school of philosophy around 300 BC, when he experienced a shipwreck that resulted in the loss of all his possessions. He told his colleagues, "Fortune bids me to philosophize with a lighter pack."[10] Life is filled with both pleasant and unpleasant events, and all of them are a part of what we experience. We don't need to like them, but we also don't need to add to our unhappiness by continuing to assess them negatively.

"Humans aren't perfect"

Another simple, but very important big truth of life is that we *humans aren't perfect*. This is guaranteed by both nature and nurture. Our genes provide us with imperfect bodies, dispositions, mental abilities, behaviors, and emotions. And if that's not enough, we pick up on beliefs, attitudes, and perspectives from family, friends, and society that can also be imperfect.

There is a bell curve to humanity, representing the reality of a diverse rainbow of human traits and personalities. If we expect people to not make mistakes and always have agreeable personalities, our social interactions will be a source of frustration and irritation. If we expect ourselves to not make mistakes, always make the right choices, and always be liked and understood, we will be unhappy and sorely disappointed.

Remembering this truth, and applying fewer judgments toward ourselves and others, is important in accepting life. Choose one or two phrases from the following list that feel natural to you, When you find yourself frustrated by a coworker, friend, family member, or yourself—especially over things that don't really matter—try one out.

- "Nobody's perfect."
- "Everyone makes mistakes."
- "Everybody's got challenges."
- "Everyone's different."
- "I don't know what it's like to walk in their shoes."
- "It's not easy being human."

In the case of truly difficult, irritating people, you can remind yourself that they are a part of life or they are who they are. (See chapter 1 for skills in assertively interacting with difficult people.)

"This just doesn't matter"

Letting things go when they don't matter is as assertive as standing up for ourselves when they do. The low-hanging fruit of acceptance is to accept those things that we have no power to change. As the Stoic philosopher Epictetus put it, "What then is to be done? To make the best of what is in our power, and take the rest as it naturally happens."[11]

Some things are quite important: protection, survival, good relationships with those we love, good mental and physical health, and our interests and causes. But so many everyday events simply aren't that important or aren't within our choice or control. What if someone cuts us off in traffic, our favorite football team wins (or loses), the weather today is hot (or cold), or a friend offended us 10 years ago—these simply don't matter in the larger scheme of things. What matters to us varies from individual to individual, depending on our personal values. But it's safe to say that we can all make mountains out of molehills by living on autopilot with our natural judgmental tendencies and habits. Despite our inherent instinct to judge (i.e., assess things as good or bad), we don't *need* to judge things that don't matter if we so choose. But not judging does require intentional mental effort.

Here are examples of the types of phrases to consider when you need to remind yourself that something doesn't matter. Develop a few go-to phrases that work best for you.

- "This just doesn't matter."
- "Some things matter, but not this."
- "What's the worst that can happen?"
- "Why does this matter?"
- "I literally can't do anything about this."
- "Will worrying make this any better?"
- "Is this worth the bother?"
- "Let it go."
- "I don't need to judge this."
- "This won't mean a thing in a hundred years."

Tool #2. Disputing Exaggerated Negative Thinking

Hopefully, one of the preceding big truths can help bring you back to a degree of helpful acceptance. But sometimes we need to drill further down into our thinking, in order to help that process. A major tenet of cognitive behavioral psychology is identifying "cognitive distortions"—flawed, inflexible thinking, based on not considering all factors—and providing useful responses to them. While there are many types of these distortions, one of the most powerful, when it comes to not accepting life, is *exaggerated negative thinking*.

Exaggerated negative thinking means thinking in simplistic, extreme, unreasonable ways about ourselves, other people, or specific situations. It can involve catastrophic thinking, all-or-nothing thinking, a sole focus on negative factors, or forecasts of only negative outcomes—all of which end up with us seeing things as worse than they really are. It fails to balance that assessment with other factors, thus not allowing us to see other perspectives. We can choose to perceive things differently by not focusing solely on what's wrong in our lives. We can balance this way of thinking, or even replace it, by putting more focus on what's right in our lives.

Table 4.1 offers some simple examples of the types of responses we can use with exaggerated negative thinking. The first crucial step is to consciously realize that we *are* exaggerating. The second is to consider other factors we've previously omitted. If you need to be more objective, imagine that you're giving advice to a family member or best friend who came to you with this type of exaggerated thinking.

In *Learned Optimism*, Martin Seligman makes the key point that optimism itself isn't as much about positive thinking as it is about *nonnegative* thinking.[12] We don't need to look in the mirror and say, "I'm the best thing ever"; we need to respond to exaggerated thoughts that say, "I'm not worthwhile." We don't need to maintain that life is "all good"; we need to remind ourselves that life is "not all bad." A helpful resource regarding additional ideas and tools for dealing with exaggerated negative thinking and other cognitive distortions is *Feeling Good*, by David Burns.[13]

Naoki teaches, practices, and researches cognitive behavioral therapy. He notes that one of its key goals is to promote more flexible, balanced thinking. This entails considering all aspects in a given situation—both the positives and the negatives. Such an approach focuses on information that is supported by facts and other evidence, rather than being based

Table 4.1 Disputing exaggerated negative thinking

Situation	Exaggerated Thinking	Rational Response
You feel very hungry	I can't stand it. I can't wait.	I'm exaggerating. It's just a sensation. It's really not that bad. It's not pleasant, but it won't kill me.
Your friend is monopolizing a conversation	She has such an ego and just goes on and on.	I'm exaggerating. She's not perfect, but she's a good friend. I can just tell her that I need to go.
Your company loses a customer	It's all my fault.	I'm exaggerating. I could have done a few things better, but there were a lot of mitigating factors. The client wasn't all that reasonable. This is part of life.
You watch a negative news story	The world is getting worse all the time.	I'm exaggerating. The world is actually better in many ways than it was a hundred years ago. I'm seeing only the bad when there's also much good.
Your significant other doesn't help you with something	She's so damned inconsiderate.	I'm exaggerating. She's not perfect, but she has so many other good qualities. If I've got a problem, I need to calm down and talk with her.
You're overweight	I've got no self-control. I feel worthless.	This is exaggerated thinking. I'm just a regular human being, without great metabolism. We're talking about being overweight, not about a character flaw.

on loose impressions and judgments. This is crucial. Once this information has been subjected to empirical scrutiny, it becomes clear that exaggerated negative thinking and unreasonable beliefs don't hold up. The more you can stick to clear-eyed facts and depend less on impressions and judgments, the more balance you can have in your thinking—and in your life generally.

Tool #3. Maintaining Core Beliefs That Promote Acceptance
Many of our thoughts, emotions, and behaviors flow from our underlying *core beliefs* (assumptions) about ourselves, others, and life. Harsh and unreasonable beliefs can be detrimental to both acceptance and our general well-being. Even if we try to counter exaggerated negative thinking, retaining flawed, exaggerated core beliefs may overwhelm our efforts to gain a better perspective.

Albert Ellis, an early advocate of cognitive behavioral techniques, and Kristene Doyle have identified three common unreasonable beliefs (they call them the "three musts") that are particularly detrimental to happiness.[14]

1. I must do well and win the approval of others, or else I'm not worthwhile.
2. Other people must do the right thing (as judged by me), or else they're not good.
3. Life must be easy, without discomfort or inconveniences.

Such musts can seriously get in the way of our well-being. They provide unreasonable expectations that will certainly lead to dissatisfaction with life. An important part of happiness is to have reasonable beliefs or expectations that correspond with how life really is. *Reasonable beliefs* are grounded in assumptions that are believable, self-evident, and in line

Table 4.2 Core beliefs that promote acceptance

Unreasonable Belief	Reasonable Belief
I'm not worthwhile if I make mistakes or I'm not liked. (Or, contrarily, I'm the greatest thing ever if I do well).	I'm not perfect, but I'm also just fine. I'm a regular, worthwhile human being, with strengths and limitations.
Other people are not good if they aren't how I want them to be.	Most people are regular humans, just like me. The world is filled with a variety of traits and personalities.
Life is mostly not OK.	There is both good and bad in the world. I can make the world a better place.
Life should be easy and fun.	There are both fun things and difficulties in life. Life requires effort.
I should be able to do whatever I want.	The world is better for everyone if we treat others as we would like to be treated.

Adapted from Scott Cooper, *Rock and Water: The Power of Thought, the Peace of Letting Go* (Camarillo, CA: DeVorss, 2017), 57.

with common sense. Table 4.2 contains a two-column list, pairing unreasonable and reasonable beliefs.

Our beliefs are influenced by both nature (our innate personalities) and nurture (family and cultural influence). As we become adults, most of us have the mental ability to intentionally review and evaluate our beliefs, to make sure they make sense to us and are good for us. It can be helpful to remind ourselves of reasonable beliefs in our everyday comings and goings, in order to develop greater acceptance in our lives.

Tool #4. Applying Nonjudgmental Awareness, or Mindfulness

Mindfulness and mindfulness meditation have been central features of Buddhism for more than two millennia. Along with traditional Buddhist teachings, a more secular version of mindfulness has become a larger feature of Western well-being practices since the 1970s. The core idea of mindfulness is fairly simple: learning to pay attention, on purpose, and without judgment. Mindfulness meditation is a formal practice to train the mind in mindfulness for everyday living. Because mindfulness is based in nonjudgmental acceptance, it directly fosters an attitude of acceptance. In fact, *mindfulness* is defined as awareness of present experience, with acceptance. Instead of using verbal responses to soften judgments, mindfulness practitioners employ nonjudgmental awareness as a direct form of acceptance, without needing to use words (although verbal cues and support can certainly be helpful). The basic principles of mindfulness are widespread and well known, but below are two practical approaches you might experiment with if you're not familiar with the technique.

1. *Mindfulness meditation.* A common, basic form of mindfulness meditation is to sit quietly and focus on your breathing, letting go of all other mental activities—including judgment—and gently returning to the inflow and outflow of air in your nostrils and belly if your mind drifts away. This simple practice can be used as a form of formal meditation on a daily basis (experiencing the ebb and flow of your breath, just as you would the ebb and flow of the ocean or the waves of a lake). It can also be used informally by returning to a neutral focus on breathing, for moments at a time, at any point in the day.
2. *Everyday mindfulness.* If you're not inclined toward formal meditation, you can still informally apply this same mindful attention to almost any daily activity:

eating, walking, listening, showering, driving, observing nature, and so forth. Not only does this develop greater nonjudgmental acceptance, but it also helps us experience life's details more fully. It helps us pay attention and be in the moment. The key is to focus on seeing and experiencing the details of life, letting go of evaluations and judgments. Focus on the details of how food tastes, of your feet hitting the ground, of water on your skin as you shower. If evaluations do enter in, accept evaluation itself, without judgment.

Wherever You Go, There You Are, by Jon Kabat-Zinn, is a helpful introduction to both formal and informal mindfulness practice.[15]

"Radical acceptance," a term used by Tara Brach and others, means incorporating acceptance into our mindset for everyday living, and also as part of our worldview. In particular, it involves letting go of our natural tendency to try to mentally control things that are out of our hands or that we cannot change. We have the power of choice in some matters, but not in others. Radical acceptance includes accepting the reality of our life—including our thoughts, emotions, and circumstances—in the moment, without judgment and with compassion. If we practice mindfulness meditation, this is a natural time to also practice radical acceptance. These are moments when we let go of mental turmoil and worry by sitting back and letting the universe simply be or, similarly, by letting God take care of the universe (placing everything "in God's hands"). From time to time, by generally accepting all that is, we can foster greater peace of mind

SELF-ACCEPTANCE

It goes without saying that to get the full benefit of accepting life, we need to accept ourselves. One of the most important realities we need to understand, for our own well-being, is that we are imperfect, but also worthwhile, *regular* human beings. *Regular* is defined here as not evil (i.e., not persistently cruel or dangerous). The vast majority of us are regular, with wonderful strengths in some areas and limitations in others. We're not perfect, but we're also not a bad person. In terms of inherent worth, one regular human is equally as valuable as another.

Regular humans have a rich variety of traits and features: body shapes and sizes, physical features, personality types, mental and physical capabilities, ages, genders, ethnicities, and cultural and religious backgrounds. But sometimes our larger social and commercial influences have disparaged differences in these features and traits, elevating some at the expense of others. Assertive self-acceptance means taking the time to remind ourselves that "we're just fine, thank you very much."

Self-acceptance also means not dwelling on our traits in overly negative ways, such as "I'm so heavy," or I'm so old," or "My nose is all wrong," or "I'm so clumsy." It also means not dwelling on past behaviors and choices in negative ways, such as "I'm a screwup" or "How could I have done that?" Regular humans make mistakes—and always will.

Self-acceptance overlaps with but isn't the same as self-compassion. *Self-compassion* means offering ourselves kindness and support. Self-acceptance is a more fundamental belief about self. It's adopting the conviction that we are worthwhile, regular humans, regardless of our shortcomings, and countering unneeded negative judgments and thoughts about ourselves.

As with any form of acceptance, this doesn't mean that we shouldn't change behaviors that are harmful or unhelpful. Self-acceptance can't be an excuse for cruel, hurtful behavior. It doesn't mean that everything we do is good or that we should like everything we do. We still need to take responsibility for our actions and make up for any harm we've done. In the same way that we can have unconditional acceptance and love for a son, daughter, other family member, or close friend—despite their flaws and shortcomings—we can apply this same level of unconditional acceptance toward ourselves. Psychologists and educators have identified self-acceptance as an important cornerstone to well-being.[16] Without this anchor, our well-being will be adrift.

Consider using the following phrase to help you maintain a clear perspective in support of self-acceptance: "I'm not perfect, just a regular human being with both strengths and limitations." This basic core truth can also be used in reference to other people if we find that we too often apply unneeded negative judgments to others.

ACCEPTANCE OF EMOTIONS

We are fundamentally mental beings, and a big part of our mental experience is the emotional activity that flows through us. Here are some important features of emotions.

1. Positive emotions not only feel good, but they can also expand and broaden our mental abilities and help us build connections with others.
2. Negative emotions don't feel good, but they get our attention and help us protect ourselves and others.

3. Emotions are not "us," any more than a physical ache or pain is. They're sensations that naturally flow through us, and they're not perfect.
4. Imperfect emotions arise in us daily and are defined herein as those emotional sensations that are unneeded, unhelpful, and unpleasant.

It would be great if we only felt guilt in order to prevent us from harming others; fear only as a way to avoid physical danger; worry only when we need to prepare for an important forthcoming event; or anger only when we need to protect ourselves and others. But this is not the case. Depending on our innate emotional predispositions and our life experiences, we may experience unpleasant, painful emotions too often or too intensely, with them occurring at times when they're completely unneeded and unhelpful. Sometimes our negative emotions are telling us something important, but at other times they are just detrimental noise.

Steven Hayes was a young professor of psychology at the University of North Carolina at Greensboro. In the middle of a departmental debate, he suddenly could not breathe or speak, felt like he was having a heart attack, and had to leave the room. This was his first panic attack, followed by two years of a downward spiral of difficulties from panic and anxiety. He tried to use traditional means of coping—counseling, self-talk, and medication—but nothing seemed to make a lasting difference. It was this personal experience that led him to develop, with others, an approach to working with difficult emotions, based on acceptance and mindfulness, called acceptance and commitment therapy (ACT). Metaphorically, ACT is about deciding to "drop the rope" in a tug-of-war with difficult emotions.[17] Some key principles coming out of this approach include the following.

1. Developing the skill of monitoring our natural feelings from the perspective of a third-party observer—that is, using the transcendental part of us that is able to observe our thoughts, emotions, and everything else. This includes stepping back and noticing details about the types and intensity of our natural emotional sensations (e.g., sharp, dull, numb, sour, pungent, fluttering, bitter, etc.).
2. Mindfully accepting unpleasant, difficult-to-change emotions with less judgment and more compassion, rather than fighting them or trying to escape from them.
3. Focusing on our relationship to our thoughts and feelings, rather than on their content. Again, this means seeing thoughts as mental sensations, rather than as self, or "me."
4. Keeping a focus on our core personal values and living a life fully committed to those values, regardless of unpleasant emotions that may come and go.

As with acceptance generally, acceptance of difficult emotions is not resignation. It's more clearly seeing feelings for what they are: natural inner sensations that may or may not be useful. Emotions are like flavors, and sometimes they really don't "taste" very good. Accepting unpleasant emotions doesn't require us to like these sensations or judge them positively. Instead of avoiding or fighting them, we strive to simply take them in, without negative judgments and reactions. Psychologists maintain that fretting over feelings of anxiety can make those emotions even more intense. *Acceptance of unpleasant emotions* involves letting them happen with fewer negative judgments.

In *The Mindfulness Solution*, professor of psychology Ronald Siegel suggests a form of meditation where we mindfully invite unpleasant emotions ("stepping into fear"), in order to become more comfortable with them.[18] Instead of breathing being the focus when we practice mindfulness, unpleasant emotional sensations become the focus of nonjudgmental awareness. Put another way, we can invite our fear to tea or out for coffee. We simply are present when such emotions occur.

Severe emotional pain, like physical pain, needs attention, including professional therapy and medical help, if necessary. But, as Steven Hayes suggests, we can also begin to develop a different, more flexible relationship with our emotions. In the spirit of ACT, the following are a few self-evident thoughts that you can use to remind yourself of the nature of our imperfect emotions (i.e., the ones that are unneeded, unhelpful, and unpleasant).

- "This emotion is a natural sensation. It's not 'me,' or 'self.'"
- "This sensation is part of life."
- "It is what it is."
- "This sensation is unpleasant, but it also doesn't matter."
- "This sensation is unpleasant, but it won't kill me."
- "I'm a regular human being, experiencing imperfect emotions."

It's clear that reducing exaggerated, negative thoughts and beliefs can help alleviate unneeded negative emotions. But nonnegative thinking (and mindfulness) cannot eliminate all natural, imperfect emotional suffering from our lives, any more than we can eliminate all physical pain. Try these:

- We can list all the rational reasons for not feeling nervous before giving a speech, yet still feel nervous about delivering it.
- When we exercise, we can mentally note that we are not currently experiencing pain yet still feel an ongoing, low-grade fear of potential pain.
- We can provide ourselves with all manner of soothing words, yet still experience a panic attack or anxiety.
- We can provide ourselves with the most rational perspectives when tragedy happens in our lives, yet still feel deep grief.

If we are born with a stronger genetic predisposition for depression, then therapy, medication, and behavioral activation can help, but we will very likely still experience depressive moods to one extent or another. Nothing will totally eliminate emotional suffering from our lives, since emotional difficulty is embedded in human existence. Even if we learn to accept these sensations with fewer negative judgments, the discomfort doesn't necessarily go away. But it is much more likely that we will be able to (1) enhance our ability to coexist with unpleasant emotions, (2) not intensify the sensations even further, and (3) get important things done (i.e., live our values), even in the midst of those sensations.

DEALING WITH ACUTE DEPRESSION ACCOMPANIED BY SUICIDAL THOUGHTS

Acceptance in no way means that we submit to *acute depression*—emotions and thoughts of an extreme and life-threatening nature—rather than urgently seeking a remedy. We would get emergency medical help (and possibly be hospitalized) if we were having a heart attack or fractured one or several bones. We need to do the same if we are experiencing acute depression, accompanied by suicidal thoughts. We do not choose these extreme emotions and thoughts, any more than we choose a serious medical condition. And our depression is not "us," any more than our broken bones are. Feelings of depression are part of our sometimes quite difficult human experience. But in extreme situations, the most crucial assertive action we need to take reverts back to our advice in chapter 1—speak up! If you are in a burning building, everything may look overwhelmingly bleak, but you still can cry out to the emergency crew just outside the building, who desperately want to help. We would not hesitate to do this when inside a burning building, and we cannot hesitate to similarly call for help in the presence of seriously suicidal intentions. If you have nowhere else to turn, immediately call your nation's emergency telephone number (e.g., 911 in the United States, and 119 in Japan).

NAVIGATING PERSONAL TRAGEDY

Some losses, mistakes, and accidents are tragic, unalterable, and out of our control. In particular, the death of a loved one can cause deep grief and suffering. Such losses can't be accepted easily, and they must run their course. Only those who have experienced the loss of a child or a spouse/partner can fully understand and authoritatively speak about the intense emotional pain that is so often caused by these events. Those of us who have not yet been compelled to travel down this path can only offer love, kindness, and friendship to those who are now called upon to bear the unbearable and walk this lonely path. From what the bereaved tell us, we know that deep pain often lies behind an outward appearance of strength. Yet it is also important to understand that these individuals do not want our pity. After all, such events can happen to any of us, at any time. We need to always remember that people who have suffered a loss do not want us to forget their loved ones. We honor those individuals best by speaking about them openly, as if they were still present.

Carol Smith, a journalist and editor for National Public Radio, wrote the following in *Psychology Today*.

> My son Christopher died on a bright New Year's Eve morning 27 years ago. He was seven—a joyful, stubborn child, who was deaf, but seldom silent. His exuberant whoops and enthusiastic signing directed my attention to all the ordinary wonders of our world. I still think about him every day, sometimes with a kind of dizzy joy and gratitude that I got to love him for his seven years. I smile whenever my lawn blooms with dandelions. "Wind flowers," he would sign to me before tugging me down to make a wish and blow. But sometimes an unexpected trigger—a friend calling with news that one of my son's old playmates has gotten married, or the sight of children playing on a slide—and it hits me with the force of a building collapsing; it's his ashes I've now scattered to the wind and no amount of wishing will bring him back.[19]

She then went on to discuss the unbounded nature of grief.

> Grief is not linear. There is no end of the line, no cutoff point. We don't stop grieving on a schedule any more

than we stop loving on one. I recently attended a conference for families who had lost children. I didn't hear a single person speak of closure. "I hate that word," said one mom, something I've heard echoed over and over in grief support rooms over the years.

Pauline Boss, a professor, grief researcher, and counselor, experienced the loss of her husband. In *The Myth of Closure*, she contends that with the loss of a treasured loved one, it's not natural, reasonable, or even possible to simply move on.[20] Why would we possibly want to move on from such memories and love? Grief is a natural response that may come and go for a lifetime. While our loved ones are physically absent from our lives, they continue to be a beloved presence in our hearts and minds. As Mitch Albom wrote, "Death ends a life, not a relationship."[21] Certain Asian, Latin American, and religious cultures have acknowledged this reality by establishing formal traditions that are focused on remembering and honoring deceased loved ones. In much of Asia, it is common for family members to go to temples on a routine basis, making offerings and prayers to and on behalf of departed loved ones. In Latin America and among some Christian communities, the Day of the Dead and All Saints Day are formally celebrated as a time to remember loved ones.

Joanne Cacciatore, another expert in the field of bereavement, lost a young child of her own. In *Bearing the Unbearable*, she suggests that we consider opening up to our grief—to both the painful suffering that accompanies it, as well as to the strong love for and memories of our loved ones that we continue to experience. Rather than fighting these aspects of our experience or trying to close them off (i.e., finding closure), we can fully accept them, without judgment.

How do we bear that which is unbearable? How do we suffer that which is insufferable? How do we endure that which is unendurable? Early grief feels wild, primitive, nonlinear, and crazed. It commands our assent and attention; it uses up all the oxygen in the room; it erupts unpredictably. Our minds replay grief-related content in habitual cycles. It feels inescapable and lasts much longer than other people, the nonbereaved, think it should. Like an open, bleeding wound it begs our tending. "I am here," grief says. "Be careful with me. Stop. Pause. Stay with me."[22]

C. S. Lewis, after losing his wife to cancer, wrote intimately about his own experience with the early stages of grief.

No one ever told me that grief felt so like fear. I am not afraid, but the sensation is like being afraid. The same fluttering in the stomach, the same restlessness, the yawning. I keep on swallowing.

At other times it feels like being mildly drunk, or concussed. There is a sort of invisible blanket between the world and me. I find it hard to take in what anyone says. Or perhaps, hard to want to take it in. It is so uninteresting.[23]

We can and should seek all the help we can get when we deeply grieve. According to experts, it may also be beneficial not to fight grief, but allow it to run its course—a course that is unique for each individual. The emotional pain (the *sensation* of grief) will be our companion for as long as necessary. Grief can't be constrained by time and space. Like love, it has no timeline and no borders.

SUMMARY OF TOOLS IN THIS CHAPTER

Big-idea perspectives: reminding yourself of core big truths to help you gain perspective, such as "It's part of life" or "Humans aren't perfect" or "This just doesn't matter."

Disputing exaggerated negative thinking: countering or challenging unneeded, exaggerated negative thoughts.

Maintaining core beliefs that promote acceptance: replacing unreasonable beliefs with more reasonable ones that are in line with common sense.

Applying nonjudgmental awareness (mindfulness): practicing formal or informal mindfulness, in order to simply observe life instead of overly assessing it.

Afterword

Happiness Research and These Four Paths

In writing this book, we were not interested in assertiveness simply for the sake of assertiveness. We were attracted by qualities that foster well-being for people in four key areas of everyday human experience: social, behavioral, emotional, and mental. In particular, we wanted our recommended tools to be supported by modern happiness research and sound psychological principles.

Over the past several decades, extensive academic research has centered on the study of happiness. There are excellent publications that provide information on these investigations for a layperson, such as *The Oxford Handbook of Happiness*, a comprehensive resource covering the outcomes of much of this academic work; *Happiness: Unlocking the Mysteries of Psychological Wealth*, by Ed Diener and Robert Biswas-Diener; and *The How of Happiness*, by Sonja Lyubomirsky. On the topic of positive emotions as a component of happiness, Barbara Fredrickson has written the helpful book *Positivity*. (These books and others are listed in Selected Bibliography.)

PSYCHOLOGICAL WEALTH

For starters, pleasure and discomfort are mental experiences, even if triggered by physical sensations. We know or experience everything through our mental faculties. Human bodies have evolved over many millennia to provide us with the instincts and abilities to physically survive on Earth. It's our advanced mental capacity, however, that provides us with the powerful ability to actually *experience* life. Even the sensations of sight, touch, smell, and taste must pass through our minds before we actually experience them.

Because we are mental beings, our well-being is also fundamentally mental. Accordingly, if we want to maintain a satisfactory level of well-being (assuming our baseline physical needs are met), we need to focus more on psychological wealth than physical wealth.[1]

The academic definition of *psychological wealth*, or happiness, is subjective well-being. It's subjective because, while some factors of well-being are common to all of us, it's also the case that well-being depends on our unique temperament, values, and cultural and social influences. The majority of researchers include two core components, in one form or another, in their definitions of *subjective well-being*: (1) life satisfaction, and (2) positive emotions.

Life Satisfaction

Life satisfaction means evaluating where we are in life, relative to where we want to be. This includes both our general satisfaction with life (on a scale of 0 to 10, how satisfied are you with your life?) and our satisfaction in specific domains (ones we value on a personal basis): family, work, income, spirituality, recreation, and others. Put simply, life satisfaction is what we *want* versus what we *have*—or, more broadly, our aspirations versus our attainments. Aspirations can come from our values and goals in life and so can be a positive motivator. If, however, we have relentless wants and expectations, then life satisfaction is more difficult to achieve. To be more satisfied, we can strive for what we want, but we can also reduce our wants and be more content with what we already have.

According to Martin Seligman, one of the pioneers in positive psychology, life satisfaction for many people involves not only enjoyment but also finding meaning (i.e., purpose) in life and being fully engaged in activities that involve our strengths and interests (i.e., flow).[2] Research undertaken by Ed Diener, one of the foremost experts on the science of happiness, convinced him that life satisfaction is a function of *doing* rather than *having*.[3] We certainly need an adequate level of material goods to achieve happiness, but above a certain amount, they don't incrementally bring greater happiness. Given this insight, a more satisfying approach to living might be to figure out first the things we want to do in life and subsequently to determine the resources we need to have in order to do those things. We don't need to follow the natural human instinct to *acquire more* simply for the sake of possessing it.

Ancient Greek philosophers, as well as modern scholars, have also promoted *eudaimonia* as a path to life satisfaction. While often translated as "happiness," a more literal translation is "living or doing well," meaning living a life of personal and civic virtue (i.e., living justly and honorably). Similarly, four to five centuries before the Common Era, Confucian scholars—notably Kongzi (Confucius) himself and his later disciple Mengzi (Mencius)—taught that the central role of benevolence and harmony was crucial for both the well-being of individuals and of society at large.

Positive Emotions

Happiness typically requires having a greater number of pleasant emotions (joy, peace, compassion, humor, confidence) than unpleasant ones (fear, worry, guilt, anger, sadness). *Positive emotions* can mean something different for a naturally low-key person (e.g., contentment, peacefulness) than for a higher-energy individual (e.g., joy, excitement). Some negative emotions are also important for our survival and well-being (fear and worry both have a practical value). Not to mention that pursuing life satisfaction sometimes entails putting up with plenty of unpleasant emotions (e.g., short-term pain for long-term gain).

A net sum of pleasant emotions—that is, on average, having more pleasant than unpleasant feelings—enhances our sense of well-being. Happiness researchers often break this emotional component of well-being into two categories: (1) having ample positive emotions (a *pleasant affect*) and (2) not having too much in the way of negative emotions (an *unpleasant affect*). To keep things simple, we're combining both of these aspects of emotional well-being into a single category. Note, however, that we can improve the *emotional* side of our well-being by engaging in those activities and strategies that increase our positive emotions or in those that decrease unneeded negative emotions.

Besides the fact that positive emotions simply feel good, research suggests that they can broaden our mental capacities, extend our social connections, and help us build reservoirs of resilience.[4] Emotions are driven by complex mental and biological relationships. Reducing unneeded negative emotions sometimes requires intentional mental and behavioral activity, including getting help from mental health professionals as well as medication (as needed).

Surveys from around the world suggest that most people are *mildly* happy. This is an average, however, and greater unhappiness exists in places with extreme poverty and disruptions.[5] Life is innately made up of joy and pain, contentment and suffering. Since this is a practical reality of life, unreasonable expectations of achieving high levels of happiness on an ongoing basis may, ironically, get in the way of our well-being. By not being more accepting of the overall mixed nature of life, we can generate unreasonable expectations and greater dissatisfaction with our lives by not having those expectations met. As French author Bernard de Fontenelle wrote, "A great obstacle to happiness is to expect too much happiness."[6]

HAPPINESS MACRO FACTORS

Sonja Lyubomirsky and other happiness experts have identified three *macro factors* that determine human happiness: (1) an inherent genetic predisposition, (2) life circumstances, and (3) intentional activities. In *The How of Happiness*, Lyubomirsky suggested a theoretical model where 50 percent of happiness is based on our natural happiness set point, 10 percent on life circumstances, and 40 percent on our intentional activities. But she and a colleague subsequently revisited this model and found that intentional activities can actually be quite variable in their impact on happiness.[7]

Since intentional activities are, after all, *intentional*, the degree of happiness we experience depends on how much we actually engage in them. Their full upside potential might be substantial, but unless we participate in such activities, we won't experience a difference in our well-being. Instead, our happiness set point will predominate. If we're born with a naturally sunny disposition, this may be just fine with us. But if we want to further enhance our well-being, the key is to intentionally take part in activities that foster satisfaction and enjoyment. Below is a discussion of these three macro factors.

Macro Factor #1. Happiness Set Point

Our *happiness set point* is the portion of our happiness that we are born with. It's the level of happiness derived from our innate personality and genetic emotional makeup. Just as we have a certain natural body weight or body temperature, we also have a natural baseline for happiness, predicated on our inherited personality traits. It's really a range rather than a point, but it can be fairly stable over time. We tend to return to this baseline of happiness, despite the temporary influence of major favorable or unfavorable life events.

For 20 years, researchers at the University of Minnesota studied a sizable sample of twins, including pairs of identical twins who had been raised apart from each other. This research was known as the Minnesota Study of Twins Raised Apart, or MISTRA. One of the findings of this research was that identical twins raised in different families were much closer to each other in terms of their personality, temperament, and level of happiness than were nonidentical twins or other children who had been raised in the very same household.[8] The correlation for levels of happiness among identical twins who were raised apart was 50 percent, compared with almost no correlation for nonidentical twins who grew up together. As a result of this and similar studies, 50 percent is often used as an approximation for the portion of our well-being that is determined by our happiness set point.[9]

With respect to innate temperament, sometimes these genetic predispositions don't appear until they are triggered by a person's environment (a phenomenon called "epigenetics"). For example, a specific gene for depression can remain relatively dormant until activated by stress or trauma.[10] Thus there is an overlap between genes (nature) and environment (nurture). At least in a few known cases, it seems as though our environment, by means of certain life events, can directly impact our genes.

In looking at the role of innate human temperaments in influencing happiness set points, scientists sometimes use the following "big five" categories of personality traits:[11]

1. openness (inventive, curious)
2. conscientiousness (efficient, organized)
3. extroversion (outgoing, energetic)
4. agreeableness (friendly, compassionate)
5. neuroticism (sensitive, nervous)

We all have these characteristics to varying degrees and in relative combinations. Each of them can be beneficial in our lives—including aspects of neuroticism, which can keep us vigilant and careful. These natural traits can also present us with challenges, such as having too much of any one of them. Some of our core attributes can remain stable from childhood through adulthood.

Even though such traits can contribute to perhaps 50 percent of our well-being, as Daniel Goleman reminds us in *Emotional Intelligence*, "temperament is not destiny."[12] Through intentional activities, we can mute tendencies that don't serve us well and consciously engage in activities that enhance our happiness. Inherently shy people can become less so by engaging in social opportunities, innately aggressive people can develop techniques to calm down, and people who are naturally melancholic can learn to counter pessimistic thoughts, engage in more active and rewarding endeavors, and get professional help as needed. All of us can intentionally spend more time on things we enjoy and less time on activities that aren't as satisfying.

Macro Factor #2. Life Circumstances

Researchers have found that, on average, approximately 10 percent of our well-being is determined by our *life circumstances* (such as income, job, health, and marital status).[13] We might assume by intuition that life circumstances would account for a much higher percentage. While it's true that good circumstances can give us short-term boosts of positive emotions, these are not always lasting. Someone who wins a lottery, falls in love, buys a new car, or spends a day at Disneyland may experience a temporary boost in happiness. Those who flunk a test, lose a home, or fall ill can have a temporary decline in happiness. But they, like all of us, tend to revert to their happiness set point.[14]

We all know examples of people who have fame, fortune, beauty, and health yet still suffer from depression. On the other hand, there are ample instances where those in difficult physical and material circumstances maintain a cheerful disposition. Buying a new home or a new car—or even winning a lottery—might increase our well-being in the short term, but it's typical to adapt to these new circumstances and return to our previous level of satisfaction or dissatisfaction. If people chase happiness by continually seeking the next new thing, they will likely find themselves on what psychologists call a "hedonic treadmill."

There are important exceptions to reverting to our happiness set point when it comes to life circumstances. Studies tell us that the death of a loved one, a severe disability, and protracted unemployment can result in a long-term drop in happiness, below our set point.[15] On the other hand, moving out of poverty and achieving income security can permanently increase our well-being (or at least raise us to our natural set point).[16]

Happiness surveys suggest the following statistical relationships between life circumstances and happiness.[17] These findings are based on averages, of course, and there are always exceptions to averages:

- There is no appreciable difference in subjective well-being based on gender.[18]
- Happiness levels remain relatively stable with age. As we age, our life satisfaction slightly increases, and both positive and negative emotions slightly decrease. Well-being tends to decline in late adulthood.[19]
- The correlation between income and well-being is moderate to small. It is strongest in moving from poverty to middle class. An income above sufficiency, however, has less impact on well-being. For this reason, even though incomes have more than doubled in the United States since World War II, happiness levels have remained virtually the same.[20]
- Religious individuals tend to be happier than nonreligious ones. Religious and spiritual practice as an *intentional activity* can increase life satisfaction in the long term.[21]

- Married people are somewhat happier than those who are single, and a *happy* marriage can result in a long-term or permanent increase. Divorce can lower levels of well-being, at least in the short term.[22]
- Health problems decrease happiness. Some research suggests, though, that even people with serious chronic disabilities (e.g., paralysis, kidney deficiency) can move in the direction of their happiness set point over time.[23]
- Unemployment can lead to lower levels of happiness.[24]

So there is some correlation between life circumstances and well-being, particularly if serious family, health, or financial events impact us in one way or another. Yet when all these circumstances are combined, they still account, on average, for approximately 10 percent of the variance in happiness. (Across studies, this number has been between 8 and 20 percent.)[25] We have a natural tendency to get used to our new circumstances and return to our happiness set point.

A note on social comparison. One form of instinctive evaluation can leave us vulnerable to short-term bursts of dissatisfaction and keep us plodding on a hedonic treadmill. *Social comparison* is a natural tendency to compare our life circumstances with those of others and feel dissatisfied with life if the comparison falls short. A meta-analysis summarizing 60-plus years of social comparison research found that people who engage in this activity generally choose to compare themselves with people whom they perceive to be better off than they are in some way (and not as much with those who are thought to be worse off), and that often results in self-deflation (i.e., less life satisfaction). This occurs with such attributes as income and physical attractiveness.[26] Social comparison is a slippery slope, as it can keep us in a dissatisfied state of always desiring more.

Macro Factor #3. Intentional Activities

This leaves *intentional activities*—what we *choose* to do and think—as the major lever we can pull to make a difference in our well-being. We cannot alter our inborn traits that predispose us to a greater or lesser level of happiness (our happiness set point). Life circumstances can make a difference, but they are not the most significant factor. Thus intentional activities are the most promising avenue for obtaining higher levels of well-being in our lives.

Of course, we, as individuals, are the only ones who truly know what we value, enjoy doing, and find satisfying, based on our unique values and interests. We are the sole judges of whether life is generally satisfying and when we are experiencing too much in the way of unpleasant emotions. Review the list of value domains in chapter 2 and see if you can decide on what you truly value, as well as which goals and activities bring you the most satisfaction and enjoyment. (You probably already know much of this intuitively.)

While beneficial activities are highly personalized, it is still useful to recognize which activities seem to lead to greater well-being for people in general. The longest-running and largest survey of life satisfaction is Germany's socio-economic panel. It has revealed that, over time, a substantial number of participants (approximately one quarter) have experienced increases in life satisfaction of 25 percent or more by prioritizing goals and activities involving altruism (e.g., helping others, activism, friendship) and/or family (e.g., a happy marriage, good relationships with their children). Participants who emphasized success-focused goals (e.g., career success, material gains) experienced almost no change in their subjective well-being over time. Similar results have come out of shorter-term British and Australian studies.[27]

Similar to the German panel results, Lyubomirsky has found that the happiest people

- commit to lifelong goals and interests,
- spend quality time with family and friends, and
- help others.

Additionally, these people tend to

- savor everyday pleasures,
- express gratitude,
- think optimistically about the future,
- develop poise and strength to cope with life's difficulties, and
- engage in physical exercise on a regular basis.[28]

Again, these are averages, not absolutes, about what provides the most life satisfaction and enjoyment. Nonetheless, we can enhance our subjective well-being by devoting more time to the types of intentional activities that bring us satisfaction and enjoyment. It's also clear that we can increase our well-being by getting the professional help we need if we are chronically unhappy.

THE FOUR PATHS AS FOUNDATIONAL GATEWAYS

Regardless of individual differences, we believe that anyone can benefit in their subjective well-being by applying the tools in the four paths of assertiveness we discussed in this book. The paths are intentional activities in and of themselves, but they are also foundational gateways to other important activities that can benefit your life.

Speaking up is a gateway to more satisfying interactions in our social worlds. By expressing what we want and how we feel, without the intent of rolling over others, we foster self-determination, problem solving, and relationship building. Our life satisfaction and level of positive emotions can be influenced by how we interact with others. Our natural emotional reaction to a social difficulty can be fight or flight (or freeze), but we are also born with the ability to use direct communication and problem solving. This not only allows us to maintain healthy and respectful relationships with others (since social connections can foster well-being), but it also helps us sustain our self-determination, including obtaining what we want out of life. We can build strong, trustworthy relationships with those close to us through direct, honest, kind communication. Ample research over the years has confirmed that this traditional form of social assertiveness contributes to both personal satisfaction and reduced anxiety.[29]

Jumping in is a gateway to many valued activities in our lives. Behavioral activation is assertively jumping in with needful or desired intentional activities, even when we don't feel like it. Life satisfaction, and the positive emotions that come with it, are not possible without jumping in. Much of our well-being is connected with *doing* more of what is personally satisfying. It's more about the journey than the place of arrival. This concept applies whether that activity is going to work, pursuing a valued goal, helping others, resting, playing a sport, socializing, or practicing mediation. Research suggests that formal behavioral activation therapy can help mitigate anxiety and depression.[30]

Embracing compassion is a gateway to responding to the most difficult emotional challenge of all: human suffering. Even if we don't always feel compassionate, we can assertively respond to both the suffering of others and our own with helpful words and actions. Compassion directly contributes to the well-being of its recipient, but there is also evidence that it benefits the provider.[31]

Accepting life is a gateway to higher levels of psychological well-being. By reducing unneeded negative judgments, acceptance increases our level of satisfaction with life and reduces the detrimental emotions that arise from too much negative evaluation. Negative judgments can lead to higher levels of frustration, anger, fear, and worry. Greater acceptance is foundational to optimism and gratitude, two core attitudes that have been linked to positive emotions. Acceptance can lead to greater resilience when dealing with life's difficulties. There is a growing body of research to support the therapeutic value of building more acceptance into our psychological lives.[32]

* * * * *

As described at the beginning of this book, full assertiveness is a much bigger concept than just speaking up. It means intentionally taking charge of our lives—socially, behaviorally, emotionally, and mentally. Our well-being depends on it. As the authors of this book, and with all best wishes, we hope that as you continue along your life's journey, you'll seriously consider the foundational assertiveness tools of *speaking up*, *jumping in*, *embracing compassion*, and *accepting life*.

NOTES

Introduction

1. Alexander Serenko, "The great resignation: The great knowledge exodus or onset of the great knowledge revolution?," *Journal of Knowledge Management* 27, no. 4 (November 2023): 1042–1055, https://doi.org/10.1108/JKM-12-2021-0920.
2. Sonja Lyubomirsky, *The How of Happiness* (New York: Penguin, 2008), 41–42.
3. Eiko Suzuki et al., "Relationship between assertiveness and burnout among nurse managers," *Japan Journal of Nursing Science* 6, no. 4 (December 2009): 71–81, https://doi.org/10.1111/j.1742-7924.2009.00124.x; Heather Spence Laschinger et al., "Workplace empowerment, incivility, and burnout: Impact on staff nurse recruitment and retention outcomes," *Journal of Nursing Management* 17, no. 3 (April 2009): 302–311, https://doi.org/10.1111/j.1365-2834.2009.00999.x.
4. World Health Organization, "Nursing and midwifery," May 3, 2024, https://www.who.int/news-room/fact-sheets/detail/nursing-and-midwifery/.

Chapter 1. Speaking Up

1. Brittany C. Speed, Brandon L. Goldstein, and Marvin R. Goldfried, "Assertiveness training: A forgotten evidence-based treatment," *Clinical Psychology: Science and Practice* 25, no.1 (March 2018): article e12216. https://doi.org/org/10.1111/cpsp.12216.
2. Rosa Parks and James Haskins, *Rosa Parks: My Story* (New York: Dial, 1992), 116.
3. James B. Parham et al., "Influences on assertiveness: gender, national culture, and ethnicity," *Journal of Management Development* 34, no. 4 (April 2015): 421–439, https://doi.org/10.1108/JMD-09-2013-0113.

4. Maggie Kuhn, *No Stone Unturned* (New York: Ballantine, 1991), 159.
5. Takashi Mitamura, "Developing the functional assertiveness scale: Measuring dimensions of objective effectiveness and pragmatic politeness," *Japanese Psychological Research* 60, no. 2 (April 2018): 63–119, https://doi.org/10.1111/jpr.12185.
6. Zhenzhong Ma and Alfred Jaeger, "A comparative study of the influence of assertiveness on negotiation outcomes in Canada and China," *Cross Cultural Management: An International Journal* 17, no. 4 (October 2010) 333–346, https://doi.org/10.1108/13527601011086568.
7. Arthur J. Lange and Patricia Jakubowski, *Responsible Assertive Behavior* (Champaign, IL: Research Press, 1976).
8. Manuel J. Smith, *When I Say No, I Feel Guilty* (New York: Bantam, 1975).
9. Viktor Frankl, *Man's Search for Meaning* (Boston: Beacon, 2006; originally published in 1946).
10. Malala Yousafzai, interview on CNN, November 2011, https://www.cnn.com/videos/world/2012/10/10/sayah-2011-interview-malala-yousufzai.cnn.
11. Arnold A. Lazarus, "On assertive behavior: A brief note," *Behavior Therapy* 4, no. 5 (October 1973): 697–699, https://doi.org/10.1016/S0005-7894(73)80161-3.
12. Andrew Salter, *Conditioned Reflex Therapy* (New York: Creative Age, 1949).
13. Alicia Keys, *More Myself* (New York: Flatiron, 2020), 118.
14. Peter Drucker, "Archivist's pick: On asking the right questions," Drucker Institute, March 27, 2014, https://drucker.institute/thedx/asking-the-right-questions.
15. Larry King, interview on CNN, December 2010, https://www.youtube.com/watch?v=PjQeGjMq9Xs.
16. Mahatma Gandhi, speech at sedition trial in Ahmedabad, India, March 18, 1922, https://www.mkgandhi.org/speeches/gto1922.htm.
17. Rudrangshu Mukherjee, ed., *The Penguin Gandhi Reader* (New York: Penguin, 1993), 134.
18. Thomas Merton, ed., *Gandhi on Non-Violence* (New York: New Directions, 1965), 29.

19. Anna Vannucci, Kaitlin M. Flannery, and Christine McCauley Ohannessian, "Social media use and anxiety in emerging adults," *Journal of Affective Disorders* 207 (January 2017): 163–166, https://doi.org/10.1016/j.jad.2016.08.040.
20. Roger Fisher, William Ury, and Bruce Patton, *Getting to Yes*, 3rd ed. (New York: Penguin, 2011).
21. Milan Dinic and Camilla Walden, "Our personalities: Do we like ourselves, are we shy and is 'British reserve' a real thing?," YouGov, November 12, 2019, https://yougov.co.uk/topics/society/articles-reports/2019/11/12/yougov-personality-study-part-one-British-reserve/.
22. Daniel W. McNeil, "Terminology and evolution of constructs related to social phobia," in S. G. Hofmann, and P. M. DiBartolo, eds., *From Social Anxiety to Social Phobia* (Boston: Allyn & Bacon, 2001), 8–19; Murray B. Stein, "Coming face-to-face with social phobia," *American Family Physician* 60 (1999): 2244–2247.
23. Renate Wagner et al., "Delays in referral of patients with social phobia, panic disorder and generalized anxiety disorder attending a specialist anxiety clinic," *Journal of Anxiety Disorders* 20, no. 3 (2006): 363–371, https://doi.org/10.1016/j.janxdis.2005.02.003.
24. Ronald M. Rapee, "Descriptive psychopathology of social phobia," in R. G. Heimberg, M. R. Liebowitz, D. A. Hope, and F. R. Schneier, eds., *Social Phobia: Diagnosis, Assessment, and Treatment* (New York: Guilford, 1995), 41–66.
25. National Institute for Health and Clinical Excellence [NICE], "Social anxiety disorder: Recognition, assessment and treatment," Clinical Guideline No. 159, May 22, 2013, https://www.nice.org.uk/guidance/cg159.
26. Naoki Yoshinaga et al., "Long-term effectiveness of cognitive therapy for refractory social anxiety disorder: One-year follow-up of a randomized controlled trial," *Psychotherapy and Psychosomatics* 88, no.4 (2019): 244–246, https://doi.org/10.1159/000500108; Naoki Yoshinaga et al., "Cognitive behavioral therapy for patients with social anxiety disorder who remain symptomatic following antidepressant treatment: A randomized, assessor-blinded,

controlled trial," *Psychotherapy and Psychosomatics* 85, no.4 (2016): 208–217, https://doi.org//10.1159/000444221.
27. David M Clark et al., "More than doubling the clinical benefit of each hour of therapist time: A randomised controlled trial of internet cognitive therapy for social anxiety disorder," *Psychological Medicine* 53, no.11 (2023): 5022–5032, https://doi.org/10.1017/S0033291722002008; Graham R. Thew et al., "Internet-delivered cognitive therapy for social anxiety disorder in Hong Kong: A randomized controlled trial," *Internet Interventions* 28 (April 2022): article 100539, https://doi.org/10.1016/j.invent.2022.100539; Naoki Yoshinaga et al., "Preliminary evaluation of translated and culturally adapted internet-delivered cognitive therapy for social anxiety disorder: Multicenter, single-arm trial in Japan," *JMIR Formative Research* 7, no. 1 (2023): e45136, https://doi.org/10.2196/45136.
28. Sina-Simone Schreier et al., "Social anxiety and social norms in individualistic and collectivistic countries," *Depression and Anxiety* 27, no. 12 (December 2010): 1128–1134, https://doi.org/10.1002/da.20746.
29. Ann Hackmann, David M. Clark, and Freda McManus, "Recurrent images and early memories in social phobia," *Behaviour Research and Therapy* 38, no. 6 (2000): 601–610, https://doi.org/10.1016/s0005-7967(99)00161-8; David A. Moscovitch et al., "Autobiographical memory retrieval and appraisal in social anxiety disorder," *Behaviour Research and Therapy* 107 (2018): 106–116, https://doi.org/10.1016/j.brat.2018.06.008.
30. Arnoud Arntz, "Imagery rescripting as a therapeutic technique: Review of clinical trials, basic studies, and research agenda," *Journal of Experimental Psychopathology* 3, no. 2 (2012): 189–208, https://doi.org/10.5127/jep.024211; Julia Kroener et al., "Imagery rescripting as a short intervention for symptoms associated with mental images in clinical disorders: A systematic review and meta-analysis," *Journal of Psychiatric Research* 166 (2023): 49–60, https://doi.org/10.1016/j.jpsychires.2023.09.010.
31. Jennifer Wild and David M. Clark. "Imagery rescripting of early traumatic memories in social phobia," *Cognitive and Behavioral*

Practice 18, no. 4 (2011): 433–443, https://doi.org/10.1016/j.cbpra
.2011.03.002.

Chapter 2. Jumping In

1. Ben Singh et al., "Effectiveness of physical activity interventions for improving depression, anxiety and distress: An overview of systematic reviews," *British Journal of Sports Medicine* 57, no.18 (2023): 1203–1209, https://doi.org/10.1136/bjsports-2022-106195.
2. Trevor Mazzucchelli, Robert Kane, and Clare Rees, "Behavioral activation treatments for depression in adults: A meta-analysis and review," *Clinical Psychology: Science and Practice* 16, no. 4 (December 2009): 383–411, https://doi.org/10.1111/j.1468-2850.2009.01178.x.
3. Sona Dimidjian et al., "Randomized trial of behavioral activation, cognitive therapy, and antidepressant medication in the acute treatment of adults with major depression," *Journal of Consulting and Clinical Psychology* 74, no. 4 (August 2006): 658–670, https://doi.org/10.1037/0022-006X.74.4.658.
4. Roy P. Basler, ed., "Letter to Mary Speed on September 27,1841," *Collected Works of Abraham Lincoln: The Abraham Lincoln Association, Springfield, Illinois* (New Brunswick, NJ: Rutgers University Press, 1953), 261.
5. Don E. Fehrenbacher, ed., *Lincoln: Speeches & Writings 1832–1858*, Library of America No. 46 (New York: Penguin Putnam, 1989), 197.
6. Drew Barrymore, interview in *Parade*, September 9, 2022, https://parade.com/celebrities/drew-barrymore-health.
7. Pim Cuijpers, Annemieke van Straten, and Lisanne Warmerdam, "Behavioral activation treatments of depression: A meta-analysis," *Clinical Psychology Review* 27, no. 3 (April 2007): 318–326, https://doi.org/10.1016/j.cpr.2006.11.001.
8. Discussed in Jonathan W. Kanter, Andrew M. Busch, and Laura C. Rusch, *Behavioral Activation* (New York: Routledge, 2009), 6–8.
9. Kelly G. Wilson et al., "The valued living questionnaire: Defining and measuring valued action within a behavioral framework," *Psychological Record* 60, no. 2 (April 2010; published June 30, 2017): 249–272, https://doi.org/10.1007/BF03395706.

10. Steven C. Hayes, Kirk D. Strosahl, and Kelly G. Wilson, *Acceptance and Commitment Therapy*, 2nd ed. (New York: Guilford, 2012), 304–307.
11. Jon Stewart on *The Daily Show*, Comedy Central, January 22, 2009.
12. Cynthia Kersey, *Unstoppable* (Naperville, IL: Sourcebooks, 1998), 78–81.
13. See, for example, Ed Diener and Robert Biswas-Diener, *Happiness: Unlocking the Mysteries of Psychological Wealth* (Malden, MA: Blackwell, 2008), and Ed Diener, Eunkook M. Suh, Richard E. Lucas, and Heidi L. Smith, "Subjective well-being: Three decades of progress," *Psychological Bulletin* 125, no. 2 (1999): 278–279, https://doi.org/10.1037/0033-2909.125.2.276.

Chapter 3. Embracing Compassion

1. Richard Carlson and Benjamin Shield, eds., *Handbook for the Spirit*, 3rd ed. (Novato, CA: New World Library, 2008), 20.
2. For a helpful review of research on children and compassion, see Tracy L. Spinard and Nancy Eisenberg, "Compassion in children," in Emma M. Seppala et al., eds., *The Oxford Handbook of Compassion Science* (New York: Oxford University Press, 2017), 53–64; Robert Hepach, Amrisha Vaish, and Michael Tomasello, "Young children are intrinsically motivated to see others helped," *Psychological Science* 23, no. 9 (September 2012): 967–972, https://doi.org/10.1177/0956797612440571.
3. David G. Rand, Joshua D. Greene, and Martin A. Nowak, "Spontaneous giving and calculated greed," *Nature* 489, no. 7416 (September 2012): 427–430, https://doi.org/10.1038/nature11467.
4. Bruce Headey, Ruud Muffels, and Gert G. Wagner, "Long-running German panel survey shows that personal and economic choices, not just genes, matter for happiness," *PNAS* [*Proceedings of the National Academy of Sciences*] 107, no. 42 (October 2010): 17922–17926, https://www.pnas.org/doi/full/10.1073/pnas.1008612107; Bruce Headey, "Set-point theory may need replacing: Death of a paradigm?," in Susan A. David, Ilona Boniwell, and Amanda

Conley Ayers, eds. *The Oxford Handbook of Happiness* (New York: Oxford University Press, 2013), 887–900.
5. Stephanie L. Brown and R. Michael Brown, "Connecting prosocial behavior to improved physical health: Contributions from the neurobiology of parenting," *Neuroscience & Biobehavioral Reviews* 55 (August 2015): 1–17, https://doi.org/10.1016/j.neubiorev.2015.04.004.
6. Jennifer L. Goetz, Dalcher Keltner, and Emiliana Simon-Thomas, "Compassion: An evolutionary analysis and empirical review," *Psychological Bulletin* 136, no. 3 (May 2010): 351–374, https://doi.org/10.1037/a0018807.
7. Paul Bloom, *Against Empathy: The Case for Rational Compassion* (New York: HarperCollins, 2016).
8. Mark H. David, "Empathy, compassion, and social relationships," in Emma M. Seppala et al., eds., *The Oxford Handbook of Compassion Science* (New York: Oxford University Press, 2017), 299–316.
9. Steven Bertoni, "Chuck Feeney: The billionaire who is trying to go broke," *Forbes*, September 18, 2012, www.forbes.com/sites/stevenbertoni/2012/09/18/chuck-feeney-the-billionaire-who-is-trying-to-go-broke/.
10. Forbes staff, "Remembering Chuck Feeney, a maverick philanthropist who became a millionaire—and gave it all away," *Forbes*, October 9, 2023, https://www.forbes.com/sites/kerryadolan/2023/10/09/former-billionaire-chuck-feeney-philanthropist-who-pioneered-giving-while-living-has-died-at-age-92/.
11. Mother Teresa, *In the Heart of the World* (Novato, CA: New World Library, 2010), 37.
12. Richard Carlson and Benjamin Shield, eds., *Handbook for the Spirit*, 3rd ed. (Novato, CA: New World Library, 2008), 142.
13. Bono [Paul David Hewson], *Surrender* (New York: Alfred E. Knopf, 2022), 482.
14. Reihō Masunaga, trans., *A Primer of Sōtō Zen: A Translation of Dōgen's* Shōbōgenzō zuimonki [*The Treasury of the True Dharma Eye: Record of Things Heard*] (Honolulu: University of Hawaii Press, 1971), 50.
15. Barbara L. Frederickson, *Positivity* (New York: Harmony, 2009).

16. Naomi I. Eisenberger and Matthew D. Lieberman, "Why rejection hurts: A common neural alarm system for physical and social pain," *Trends in Cognitive Sciences* 8, no. 7 (July 2004): 294–300, https://doi.org/10.1016/j.tics.2004.05.010.
17. John Mordechai Gottman, *What Predicts Divorce? The Relationship between Marital Processes and Marital Outcomes* (New York: Psychology Press, 1994).
18. Marcial Losada and Emily Heaphy, "The role of positivity and connectivity in the performance of business teams: A nonlinear dynamics model," *American Behavioral Scientist* 47, no. 6 (February 2004): 740–765, https://doi.org/10.1177/0002764203260208.
19. Quotation in Elizabeth Bryan and Angela Daffron, *Soul Models* (Deerfield Beach, FL: Health Communications,), 172.
20. Alea C. Swara, Brandon G. King, and Clifford Saron, "Studies of training compassion: What have we learned; What remains unknown?," in Emma M. Seppala et al., eds. *The Oxford Handbook of Compassion Science* (New York: Oxford University Press, 2017), 219–236.
21. Helen Y. Weng, Brianna Schuyler, and Richard J. Davidson, "The impact of compassion meditation on the brain and prosocial behavior," in Emma M. Seppala et al., eds., *The Oxford Handbook of Compassion Science* (New York: Oxford University Press, 2017), 133–146.
22. Jack Kornfield, "Meditation on compassion," Jack's Teachings, jackkornfield.com, July 23, 2017, https://jackkornfield.com/meditation-on-compassion.
23. Kristen Neff, *Self-Compassion* (New York: William Morrow, 2011).
24. Ellen R. Albertson, Kristen D. Neff, and Karen E Dill-Shackleford, "Self-compassion and body dissatisfaction in women: A randomized controlled trial of a brief meditation intervention," *Mindfulness* 6 (2015): 444–454, https://doi.org/10.1007/s12671-014-0277-3; Kristin D. Neff and Christopher K. Germer, "A pilot study and randomized controlled trial of the mindful self-compassion program," *Journal of Clinical Psychology* 69, no.1 (January 2013): 28–44, https://doi.org/10.1002/jclp.21923.

25. While this quotation is widely attributed to philosopher Edmund Burke, its origin is debated.
26. Nelson Mandela, *Notes to the Future: Words of Wisdom* (New York: Atria, 2012), 84.
27. Sara B. Algoe and Jonathan Haidt, "Witnessing excellence in action: The 'other-praising' emotions of elevation, admiration, and gratitude," *Journal of Positive Psychology* 4, no. 2 (2009): 105–127, https://doi.org/10.1080/17439760802650519; Simone Schnall, Jean Roper, and Daniel M. T. Fessler, "Elevation leads to altruistic behavior," *Psychological Science* 21, no. 3 (March 2010): 315–320, https://doi.org/10.1177/0956797609359882.

Chapter 4. Accepting Life

1. J. J. van der Leeuw, *The Conquest of Illusion* (Wheaton, IL: Theosophical, 1928), 17.
2. Eleanor Roosevelt, *You Learn by Living* (New York: Harper & Brothers, 1960), foreword.
3. Michael J. Fox, *A Lucky Man* (New York: Hachette, 2003).
4. Nick Miller, "Staying positive [is] the Fox mantra for battling illness," *Sydney Morning Herald*, May 26, 2012, https://www.smh.com.au/world/staying-positive-the-fox-mantra-for-battling-illness-20120525-1zao0s.html.
5. Aili Nahas, "Michael J. Fox opens up about his health, life with Tracy Pollan: 'I'm in a really good groove,'" *People*, October 20, 2021, https://people.com/tv/michael-j-fox-opens-up-health-beautiful-life-with-wife-tracy-pollan/.
6. Andrew C. Butler et al., "The empirical status of cognitive-behavioral therapy: A review of meta-analyses," *Clinical Psychology Review* 26, no.1 (January 2006): 17–31, https://doi.org/10.1016/j.cpr.2005.07.003; Andrew T. Gloster et al., "The empirical status of acceptance and commitment therapy: A review of meta-analyses," *Journal of Contextual Behavioral Science* 18, no. 1 (October 2020): 181–192, https://doi.org/10.1016/j.jcbs.2020.09.009.
7. Amanda J. Shallcross et al., "Getting better with age: The relationship between age, acceptance, and negative affect," *Journal of*

Personality and Social Psychology, 104, no. 4 (April 2013): 734–749, https://doi.org/10.1037/a0031180.
8. Martha J. Falkenstein and David A. F. Haaga, "Measuring and characterizing unconditional self-acceptance," in Michael E. Bernard, ed., *The Strength of Self-Acceptance: Theory, Practice and Research* (New York: Springer, 2013), 139–151.
9. Suzanne Lander, *Audrey Hepburn: A Photographic Celebration*, reprint (New York: Skyhorse, 2014), 274.
10. Quotation in Moses Hadas, trans., *Stoic Philosophy of Seneca: Essays and Letters* (New York: W. W. Norton, 1968), 100.
11. Christopher Gill, ed., and Robin Hard, trans., *The Discourses of Epictetus* (London: Everyman, 1995), 6.
12. Martin Seligman, *Learned Optimism* (repr., New York: Vintage, 2005).
13. David D. Burns, *Feeling Good: The New Mood Therapy*, reprint (New York: William Morrow, 1999).
14. Albert Ellis and Kristene A. Doyle, *How to Control Your Anxiety before It Controls You*, reprint (New York: Citadel, 2016), 36–42.
15. Jon Kabat-Zinn, *Wherever You Go, There You Are*, 11th ed. (New York: Hachette Go, 2023).
16. Michael E. Bernard, ed., *The Strength of Self-Acceptance: Theory, Practice and Research* (New York: Springer, 2013).
17. For more detail on Hayes's personal journey, see Steven C. Hayes, *A Liberated Mind* (New York: Avery, 2019), 29–43; the "dropping the rope" metaphor is in Hayes, *A Liberated Mind*, 104.
18. Ronald D. Siegel, *The Mindfulness Solution* (New York: Guilford, 2010), 118–120.
19. Carol Smith, "The myth of closure: We need a better way to think about grieving," *Psychology Today*, July 26, 2021, https://www.psychologytoday.com/us/blog/writing-between-the-lines/202107/the-myth-closure/.
20. Pauline Boss, *The Myth of Closure* (New York: W. W. Norton, 2022).
21. Mitch Albom, *Tuesdays with Morrie* (New York: Doubleday, 1997), 174.
22. Joanne Cacciatore, *Bearing the Unbearable* (Somerville, MA: Wisdom, 2017), 43.

23. C. S. Lewis, *A Grief Observed* (San Francisco: HarperOne, 2015; originally published in 1961), 3.

Afterword

1. Ed Diener and Robert Biswas-Diener, *Happiness: Unlocking the Mysteries of Psychological Wealth* (Malden, MA: Blackwell, 2008), 13–26.
2. Martin Seligman, *Authentic Happiness* (New York: Free Press), 2002.
3. Diener and Biswas-Diener, *Happiness*, 13–26.
4. Anne M. Conway et al., "The broaden-and-build theory of positive emotions: Form, function, and mechanisms," in Susan A. David, Ilona Boniwell, and Amanda Conley Ayers, eds., *The Oxford Handbook of Happiness* (New York: Oxford University Press, 2013), 17–34.
5. Diener and Biswas-Diener, *Happiness*, 129–130, 142–143.
6. Quotation in Andy Zubko, ed., *Treasury of Spiritual Wisdom* (San Diego: Blue Dove, 1996), 226.
7. Sonja Lyubomirsky, *The How of Happiness* (New York: Penguin, 2008); Kevin M. Sheldon and Sonja Lyubomirsky, "Revisiting the sustainable happiness model and pie chart: Can happiness be successfully pursued?," *Journal of Positive Psychology* 16, no. 2 (2021): 145–154, https://doi.org/10.1080/17439760.2019.1689421.
8. Diener and Biswas-Diener, *Happiness*, 147–149; for a full description of MISTRA, see Nancy L. Segal, *Born Together—Reared Apart* (Cambridge, MA: Harvard University Press, 2012).
9. William Pavot and Ed Diener, "Happiness experienced: The science of subjective well-being," in Susan A. David, Ilona Boniwell, and Amanda Conley Ayers, eds., *The Oxford Handbook of Happiness* (New York: Oxford University Press, 2013), 143.
10. Sonja Lyubomirsky, *The How of Happiness* (New York: Penguin, 2008), 59–60.
11. Brian P. O'Connor, "A quantitative review of the comprehensiveness of the five-factor model in relation to popular personality inventories," *Assessment* 9, no. 2 (July 2002): 188–203, https://doi.org/10.1177/1073191102092010.

12. Daniel Goleman, *Emotional Intelligence* (New York: Bantam, 1995), 215–228.
13. Lyubomirsky, *The How of Happiness*, 41–42; Ed Diener et al., "Subjective well-being: Three decades of progress," *Psychological Bulletin* 125, no. 2 (1999): 278–279, https://doi.org/10.1037/0033-2909.125.2.276.
14. Diener and Biswas-Diener, *Happiness*, 151–161.
15. Diener and Biswas-Diener, *Happiness*, 156–161.
16. Ed Diener, Weiting Ng, and Will Tov, "Balance in life and declining utility of diverse resources," *Applied Research in Quality of Life* 3, no. 4 (2008): 277–291, https://doi.org/10.1007/s11482-009-9062-1.
17. For summaries of these types of correlations, see Lyubomirsky, *The How of Happiness*, 41–52, and Pavot and Diener, "Happiness Experienced," 134–151.
18. Pavot and Diener, "Happiness Experienced," 140.
19. For more details on the relationship between happiness and age, see Susanne Buecker et al., "The development of subjective well-being across the life span: A meta-analytic review of longitudinal studies," *Psychological Bulletin* 149 (2023): 418–446, https://doi.org/10.1037/bul0000401.
20. Diener and Biswas-Diener, *Happiness*, 91–111; Pavot and Diener, "Happiness Experienced," 141.
21. For more details on the relationship between happiness and religious engagement, see Diener and Biswas-Diener, *Happiness*, 112–126.
22. Diener and Biswas-Diener, *Happiness*, 55–57, 155–156.
23. Lyubomirsky, *The How of Happiness*, 51–52.
24. Diener and Biswas-Diener, *Happiness*, 159–160.
25. Diener et al., "Subjective well-being," 278–279.
26. J. P. Gerber, Ladd Wheeler, and Jerry Suis, "A social comparison meta-analysis 60+ years on," *Psychological Bulletin*, 144, no. 2 (2018): 177–197, https://doi.org/10.1037/bul0000127.
27. Bruce Headey, Ruud Muffels, and Gert G. Wagner, "Long-running German panel survey shows that personal and economic choices, not just genes, matter for happiness," *PNAS* [*Proceedings of the National Academy of Sciences*] 107, no. 42 (October 2010): 17922–17926,

https://doi.org/10.1073/pnas.1008612107; Bruce Headey, "Set-point theory may need replacing: Death of a paradigm?," in Susan A. David, Ilona Boniwell, and Amanda Conley Ayers, eds., *The Oxford Handbook of Happiness* (New York: Oxford University Press, 2013), 887–900.

28. Lyubomirsky, *The How of Happiness*, 22, 23, 133–136.
29. Brittany C. Speed, Brandon L. Goldstein, and Marvin R. Goldfried, "Assertiveness training: A forgotten evidence-based treatment," *Clinical Psychology: Science and Practice* 25, no.1 (March 2018): article e12216, https://doi.org/10.1111/cpsp.12216.
30. Trevor Mazzucchelli, Robert Kane, and Clare Rees, "Behavioral activation treatments for depression in adults: A meta-analysis and review," *Clinical Psychology: Science and Practice* 16, no. 4 (December 2009): 383–411.
31. Stephanie L. Brown and R. Michael Brown, "Connecting prosocial behavior to improved physical health: Contributions from the neurobiology of parenting," *Neuroscience & Biobehavioral Reviews* 55 (August 2015): 1–17, https://doi.org/10.1016/j.neubiorev.2015.04.004.
32. Andrew T. Gloster et al., "The empirical status of acceptance and commitment therapy: A review of meta-analyses," *Journal of Contextual Behavioral Science* 18, no. 1 (October 2020): 181–192, https://doi.org/10.1016/j.jcbs.2020.09.009.

SELECTED BIBLIOGRAPHY

Beck, Judith S. *Cognitive Behavior Therapy: The Basics and Beyond*. 2nd ed. New York: Guilford, 2011.

Bernard, Michael E., ed. *The Strength of Self-Acceptance: Theory, Practice and Research*. New York: Springer, 2013.

Bloom, Paul. *Against Empathy: The Case for Rational Compassion*. New York: HarperCollins, 2016.

Boss, Pauline. *The Myth of Closure*. New York: W. W. Norton, 2022.

Burns, David D. *Feeling Good: The New Mood Therapy*. Reprint. New York: William Morrow, 1999.

Butler, Andrew C., Jason E. Chapman, Evan M. Forman, and Aaron T. Beck. "The empirical status of cognitive-behavioral therapy: A review of meta-analyses." *Clinical Psychology Review* 26, no. 1 (January 2006): 17–31. https://doi.org/10.1016/j.cpr.2005.07.003.

Cacciatore, Joanne. *Bearing the Unbearable*. Somerville, MA: Wisdom, 2017.

Cooper, Scott. *Speak Up and Get Along!* 2nd ed. Minneapolis: Free Spirit, 2019.

David, Susan A., Ilona Boniwell, and Amanda Conley Ayers, eds. *The Oxford Handbook of Happiness*. New York: Oxford University Press, 2013.

Diener, Ed, and Robert Biswas-Diener. *Happiness: Unlocking the Mysteries of Psychological Wealth*. Malden, MA: Blackwell, 2008.

Diener, Ed, Eunkook M. Suh, Richard E. Lucas, and Heidi L. Smith. "Subjective well-being: Three decades of progress." *Psychological Bulletin* 125, no. 2 (1999): 278–279. https://doi.org/10.1037/0033-2909.125.2.276.

Fisher, Roger, William Ury, and Bruce Patton. *Getting to Yes*. 3rd ed. New York: Penguin, 2011.

Frankl, Viktor. *Man's Search for Meaning*. Boston: Beacon, 2006; originally published in 1946.

Frederickson, Barbara. *Positivity*. New York: Harmony, 2009.

Gloster, Andrew T., Naomi Walder, Michael A. Levin, Michael P. Twohig, and Maria Karekla. "The empirical status of acceptance and commitment therapy: A review of meta-analyses," *Journal of Contextual Behavioral Science* 18, no. 1 (October 2020): 181–192. https://doi.org/10.1016/j.jcbs.2020.09.009.

Goleman, Daniel. *Emotional Intelligence*. New York: Bantam, 1995.

Hayes, Steven C., Victoria M. Follette, and Marsha M. Linehan. *Mindfulness and Acceptance*. New York: Guilford, 2004.

Hayes, Steven C., Kirk D. Strosahl, and Kelly G. Wilson. *Acceptance and Commitment Therapy*. 2nd ed. New York: Guilford, 2012.

Headey, Bruce, Ruud Muffels, and Gert G. Wagner. "Long-running German panel survey shows that personal and economic choices, not just genes, matter for happiness." *PNAS* [*Proceedings of the National Academy of Sciences*] 107, no. 42 (October 2010): 17922–17926. https://doi.org/10.1073/pnas.1008612107.

Kabat-Zinn, Jon. *Full Catastrophe Living*. Rev. ed. New York: Bantam, 2013.

Kabat-Zinn, Jon. *Wherever You Go, There You Are*. 11th ed. New York: Hachette Go, 2023.

Kanter, Jonathan W., Andrew M. Busch, and Laura C. Rusch. *Behavioral Activation*. New York: Routledge, 2009.

Lange, Arthur J., and Patricia Jakubowski. *Responsible Assertive Behavior*. Champaign, IL: Research Press, 1978.

Lyubomirsky, Sonja. *The How of Happiness*. New York: Penguin, 2008.

Mazzucchelli, Trevor, Robert Kane, and Clare Rees. "Behavioral activation treatments for depression in adults: A meta-analysis and review." *Clinical Psychology: Science and Practice* 16, no. 4 (December 2009): 383–411. https://doi.org/10.1111/j.1468-2850.2009.01178.x.

Neff, Kristen. *Self-Compassion*. New York: William Morrow, 2011.

Seligman, Martin. *Learned Optimism*. Reprint, New York: Vintage, 2006.

Seppala, Emma M., Emiliana Simon-Thomas, Stephanie L. Brown, Monica C. Worline, C. Daryl Cameron, and James R. Doty, eds. *The Oxford Handbook of Compassion Science*. New York: Oxford University Press, 2017.

Sheldon, Kennon M., and Sonja Lybomirsky. "Revisiting the sustainable happiness model and pie chart: Can happiness be successfully pursued?" *Journal of Positive Psychology* 16, no. 2 (2021): 145–154. https://doi.org/10.1080/17439760.2019.1689421.

Siegel, Ronald D. *The Mindfulness Solution*. New York: Guilford, 2010.
Smith, Manuel J. *When I Say No, I Feel Guilty*. New York: Bantam, 1975.
Speed, Brittany C., Brandon L. Goldstein, and Marvin R. Goldfried. "Assertiveness training: A forgotten evidence-based treatment." *Clinical Psychology: Science and Practice* 25, no. 1 (March 2018): article e12216. https://doi.org/10.1111/cpsp.12216.
Williams, John C., and Steven Jay Lynn. "Acceptance: An historical and conceptual review." *Imagination, Cognition and Personality* 30, no. 1 (September 2010): 5–56. https://doi.org/10.2190/IC.30.1.c.
Yoshinaga, Naoki, Y. Nakamura, H. Tanoue, F. MacLiam, K. Aoishi, and Y. Shiraishi. "Is modified brief assertiveness training for nurses effective? A single-group study with long-term follow-up." *Journal of Nursing Management* 26, no. 1 (January 2018): 59–65. https://doi.org/10.1111/jonm.12521.

INDEX

acceptance and commitment therapy (ACT), 115–16, 117
acceptance-mindfulness practice, 10
acceptance of life (mental assertiveness), 1, 3, 5, 12; acceptance of emotions, 114–18; case examples, 97–98, 100–101; definition, 4, 6, 96, 101; differentiated from resignation, 101; effect on negative emotions, 6, 99, 115–18, 137; during personal tragedies, 119–22; as radical acceptance, 112. *See also* self-acceptance
acceptance-of-life tools: acceptance-promoting core beliefs, 102, 109–10, 123; "big idea" perspectives, 102–6, 123; disputing exaggerated negative thinking, 102, 106–9, 117, 123; nonjudgmental awareness / mindfulness, 102, 110–12, 123
acceptance-promoting core beliefs tool, 102, 109–10, 123
action lists, 63–66, 76
activity scheduling tool, 63–66, 76
aggression, 14, 19–20, 93, 131
agreeableness, 130
Albom, Mitch, 121
Allan, Robyn, 73–74
anger, 13, 14, 94, 115, 127, 137
anger management tools: cool down, 45–46, 55; *I*-statements, 25
anxiety, 50, 53, 77, 78, 115, 118. *See also* social anxiety
anxiety management tools, 14; acceptance of life, 6, 99, 115–16; "big idea" perspectives, 102; jumping in, 4, 136–37; physical activity, 56; professional assistance, 53; speaking up, 6, 136
aspirations, *vs.* attainments, 125–26
assertive individuals, stereotypes, 18
assertiveness, 1–7; benefits, 8–9; definitions, 1, 12, 21; differentiated from aggression, 14; four paths of, 1, 3, 135–37; functional, 18–20, 27–28; gender factors, 16–17; race/ethnicity factors, 16–17
assertiveness tools, 1, 5, 8–9; range of approaches, 18–20; research in, 8–12, 14, 16–17; self-growth approach, 11; traditional, 1, 12; for young people, 9–10. *See also* intentional assertiveness activities
assertiveness-training programs, 11
attachment needs, 17
avoidance behavior: jumping in alternative, 56, 66; toward dangerous situations, 35–36, 46

Barrymore, Drew, 65–66
behavioral activation. *See* jumping in
behavioral boundaries, 26
behavioral psychology, 23–24, 57–58. *See also* cognitive behavioral techniques/therapy (CBT)
behavioral well-being, 1, 87, 124
behavioral worlds, 1, 3, 10
bereavement, 57–58, 78, 97, 119–22, 132

"big idea" perspectives tool, 102–6, 123
"Bill of Assertive Human Rights," 21–23
Biswas-Diener, Robert, *Unlocking the Mysteries of Psychological Wealth*, 124
Black Americans, assertive behavior, 16–17, 18
blame, 25; as manipulation, 32, 40; mea culpa response, 40–41; no-way response, 41–42
Bloom, Paul, 80–81
body judgments, 92–93, 113, 133
Bono (Paul David Hewson), 84–85
Boss, Pauline, *The Myth of Closure*, 121
Brach, Tara, 112
Buddhism, 88, 90, 110–11
Buffett, Warren, 82–83
bullying, 9, 38–39, 52–53
Burns, David, *Feeling Good*, 107
but-twists tool, 61–63, 76

Cacciatore, Joanne, *Bearing the Unbearable*, 121–22
calendars, 65, 76
Canadian Broadcast Corporation, 97
caregivers, 79
CBT. *See* cognitive behavioral techniques/therapy (CBT)
children: behavioral boundaries, 26; death, 119–22; helping behaviors in, 78–79; suffering experienced by, 77. *See also* parents
choice, as personal right, 21–23, 72
civil rights movement, 15–17, 18; in South Africa, 93–94
coercion, 32
cognitive behavioral techniques/therapy (CBT), 6, 10–12, 52, 63–64, 66, 99, 102, 106, 107, 109
cognitive distortions. *See* thoughts/thinking, exaggerated negative
collectivism, 52
communication, assertive: continuum, 20; as direct, honest, and respectful, 6, 9, 11, 13, 19, 42, 136; investigative questions tool, 47–48, 55; kind communication tool, 49–50, 55; between parents and children, 86–87; positive communication tool, 85–87, 95; trauma as obstacle to, 52–54. *See also* speaking up (social assertiveness)
compassion (emotional assertiveness), 1, 3, 5, 12, 71, 130, 137; compassion-based mediations tool, 87–90, 95; definition, 4, 6, 80; effect on emotions, 6; effect on happiness / subjective well-being, 137; heroic, 93–95; as human instinct, 78–79, 80; jumping in and helping tool, 83–85, 95; positive communication tool, 85–87, 95; rational compassion tool, 80–83, 95; self-compassion, 91–93. *See also* empathy; sympathy
compliments, 50, 85, 86
conflict resolution, 8, 9, 14, 32, 43–46; cool down tool, 45–46, 55; solution-focused statements tool, 43–44; workable solutions tool, 43–45, 55
Confucianism, 126–27
conscientiousness, 130
contentment, 6, 126, 127, 128

conversational skills, 23; investigative questions, 47–48, 55
Coolidge, Calvin, 46
Cooper, Scott, 8–10, 43, 75, 84; *Speak Up and Get Along!*, 9, 23–24, 62; *Sticks and Stones*, 9, 62
core beliefs (assumptions), reasonable and unreasonable, 102, 109–10, 123
COVID-19 pandemic, "great resignation," 2
criticism, 32, 40–42; constructive, 86; mea culpa response, 40–41, 55; no-way response, 41–42, 55; self-criticism, 91–92
cruelty, 9, 14, 32, 33, 38–39, 70, 93, 97, 113
cultural factors: in assertiveness, 18–20, 27–28; in bereavement practices, 121; in compassion, 94–95; in happiness / subjective well-being, 125; in negative emotions, 77; in social anxiety, 52; in values, 71–72

daily action lists, 63–66
Dalai Lama, 78
Davis, Mark H., 82
decision-making ladder, 30
depression, 4, 6, 14, 53, 77, 97–98; acute, with suicidal thoughts, 118–19; genetic factors, 58, 118, 130, 131; immobilizing effect, 57–58; situational factors, 57–58
depression management tools: acceptance of life, 6; antidepressant therapy, 6, 57, 60; compassion/self-compassion, 6, 92–93; jumping in, 4, 6, 56, 57–59, 60, 63–66, 136–37; physical exercise, 56; professional mental health therapy, 53, 60, 118–19; speaking up, 6, 14; therapeutic rest, 60–61
desires, expression of, 23
Diener, Ed, 75–76, 126; *Unlocking the Mysteries of Psychological Wealth*, 124
difficult people, interactions with. *See* speaking up (social assertiveness)
dishonesty, 32, 42, 70, 81
disrespect, 17, 33
domestic violence, 39
Doyle, Kristene, 109
Drucker, Peter, 28
Dyer, Wayne, *Pulling Your Own Strings*, 8

Ellis, Albert, 109
emotional assertiveness. *See* compassion
emotional well-being, 1, 124, 127–28
emotional worlds, 1, 2, 3, 10
emotions: acceptance of, 114–18; expression of, 23; innate predispositions for, 115; perfect and imperfect, 115; relation to behavior and thoughts, 56, 57, 59–60, 102; relation to rational compassion, 80–81; relation to suffering, 77. *See also* negative emotions; positive emotions; *and specific emotions*
empathy, 80–82, 84, 91
enjoyment, role in life satisfaction, 74–76
environmental values, 70, 75
epigenetics, 130
ethics, 67, 69, 70–71
ethnicity, relation to assertive behavior, 16–17
eudaimonia, 126
exaggeration, as manipulation, 32

experience: as happiness / subjective well-being component, 126; as purpose of life, 96–98, 125
extroversion, 130

fair treatment, 3–4
fear, 77, 96, 127; CBT-based modification, 12; comparison with grief, 122; immobilizing effect, 57; instinctual/protective, 13, 14, 115; as manipulation, 32; negative emotions–based, 53, 78; negative judgment–based, 137; of non-acceptance, 17–18; of others' opinions, 18; of pain, 118; as shyness component, 50; as social anxiety component, 50; "stepping into fear" meditation, 117; trauma-related, 53
Feeney, Chuck, 82–83
Fisher, Roger, 44–45
flight-or-fight reaction, 8, 13, 14, 136
Fontenelle, Bernard de, 128
Fox, Michael J., 97–98, 101; *Lucky Man*, 97–98
Frankl, Viktor, 22
Fredrickson, Barbara, 85; *Positivity*, 124

Gandhi, Mahatma, 18, 30–32
Gates, Bill, 82–83
gender: relation to assertive behavior, 16–17; relation to happiness / subjective well-being, 132
genetic predisposition: for depression, 58, 118, 130, 131; for happiness, 3, 128–31, 134
Getting to Yes, 44

Giving Pledge, 82–83
golden rule, 81, 91
Goleman, Daniel, *Emotional Intelligence*, 130–31
Gottman, John, 86
gratitude, 27–28, 34, 86, 120, 135, 137
Gray Panthers, 18
grief, 77, 78, 87, 97, 118; bereavement-related, 87, 119–22
Griffith, Mary, *Soul Models*, 86
guilt, 8, 9, 14, 86, 115, 127; guilt-inducing language, 14, 25–26; as manipulation, 8, 21–22, 26, 32, 34, 36; silence as acknowledgment of, 41

happiness research, 2, 3, 6, 46–47, 75–76, 85; information on, 124; and life satisfaction, 125–27; on macro factors, 128–35; on positive emotions, 127–28
happiness / subjective well-being, 1; definition and components, 3, 125–28; effect of intentional activities on, 3, 128–29, 134–35; effect of interpersonal relationships on, 46–47; effect of life circumstances on, 3, 131–34; lifespan trends, 132; as psychological wealth, 75–76, 125–28; set point, 3, 128–31, 134; twin studies of, 129–30; unreasonable expectations of, 128. *See also* life satisfaction; positive emotions
Harvard Negotiation Project, 44–45
Hayes, Steven, 115–16, 117
health care professionals, 11, 80–81, 84
health status, effect on happiness, 133

INDEX

Heaphy, Emily, 86
hedonic treadmill, 131–32, 133
helplessness, 62
Hepburn, Audrey, 100–101
heroism, 93–95
homosexuality, 86–87
honesty, 33, 70; in assertiveness, 21; in communication, 6, 9, 19, 42, 48, 52–53, 136; in functional assertiveness, 20; in self-disclosure, 24, 27, 33, 48–49; in self-expression, 22–23
human experience / humanity, 124; "Bill of Assertive Human Rights," 21–23; humans as social beings, 17–18; imperfect yet worthwhile perspective, 104–5, 108, 109, 113–14, 117, 123; optimistic attitude toward, 94; role of kindness in, 50, 88; shared/common humanity, 78–79, 91–92
"humans aren't perfect" perspective, 104–5, 108, 109, 113–14, 117, 123

"I don't know/understand," as assertive right, 22, 28, 29
imagery rescripting, 53–54
individualism, 52
inertia, overcoming of. *See* jumping in
intentional assertiveness activities: definition, 3, 10; effect on happiness / subjective well-being, 3, 128–29, 134–35; religiosity as, 132. *See also* acceptance of life; compassion; jumping in; speaking up
internet, 12, 39–40, 52, 76
interpersonal relationships: influence on happiness / subjective well-being, 46–47, 136; as stress cause, 11. *See also* speaking up

introversion, 46
I-statements, 23–26, 27, 33, 34, 35
"It's part of life" perspective, 103–4, 123

Jacobsen, Neil, 66
Jakubowski, Patricia, 21
judging, 105–6. *See also* negative judgments
jumping in (behavioral assertiveness), 1, 3, 5, 6; active rest tool, 60–61; activity scheduling tool, 63–66, 76; applied to compassionate actions, 83–85, 95; *but*-twists tool, 61–63, 76; definition, 4, 6, 56, 136; effect on negative emotions, 6, 57–61, 136–37; living our values tool, 66–76; motivation based on, 59–60, 83; professional medical-based approach, 60, 66; relation to CBT, 66
jumping in and helping tool, 83–85

Kabat-Zinn, Jon, *Wherever You Go, There You Are*, 112
Kersey, Cynthia, *Unstoppable*, 73–74
Keys, Alicia, 27
kindness, 6, 70, 71, 100, 120; communication of, 49–50, 55, 86; heroic, 93; mediation based on, 88–90; self-kindness, 91, 113
King, Larry, 28–29
King, Martin Luther, Jr., 16
Kongzi (Confucius), 126–27
Kornfield, Jack, 90
Kristofferson, Kris, 72
Kuhn, Maggie, 18

Lange, Arthur, 21
Lazarus, Arnold, 23

Leeuw, J. J. van der, 96
Lewis, C. S., 122
LGBTQ+ community, 86–87
life: purpose of, 96–98, 125, 126; taking control of, 1, 2. *See also* acceptance of life
life circumstances, effect on happiness / subjective well-being, 3, 131–34
life satisfaction, 3, 4, 5, 6, 12, 64, 74, 125–27; acceptance of life–based, 6; altruism-based, 79, 134–35; compassion-based, 6; definition, 125–26; jumping in–based, 6, 74–75, 136; lifespan trends, 132; philosophies of, 126–27; relation to happiness / subjective well-being, 3, 125–27; religious/spiritual practice–based, 132; self-compassion–based, 92–93; socio-economic panel survey, 134–35; speaking up–based, 6, 13–14, 136
Lincoln, Abraham, 58–59, 62–63, 72
listening skills: compassionate, 84; mindful, 112–13; reflective, 47
living our values tool, 66–76
Losada, Marcial, 86
love, 6, 26, 79, 89, 96, 97, 119–20; Dalai Lama on, 78; for deceased loved ones, 120, 121, 122; Mother Teresa on, 83; as self-disclosure, 49; self-love, 92; unconditional, 87, 92, 114
Lyubomirsky, Sonja, *The How of Happiness*, 124, 128, 135

Mandela, Nelson (Rolihlahla), 18, 93–94
manipulation management tools, 21–22, 32–40; *I*-statements, 25–26, 33; *maybe*-phrasing ("fogging"), 36, 37, 39, 54; rational compassion, 81; shrugging (verbal or nonverbal), 33–34, 54; *you*-statements, 36–38, 37, 39, 54
marital status, effect on happiness, 133
maybe-phrasing ("fogging") tool, 36, 37, 54
mea culpa tool, 40–41, 42, 55
mediation, 136; compassion, 89–90; compassion-based, 87–90, 95; loving-kindness, 88–89; mindfulness-based, 50, 87, 89–90, 110–12, 117
melancholy, 58–59, 131
memories, 52–54, 61, 77–78, 121
Mengzi (Mencius), 126–27
mental assertiveness. *See* acceptance of life
mental well-being, 1, 124
mental worlds, 1, 2, 3, 10
meta-analyses, 6, 14
mindfulness, 92; for development of acceptance, 10, 102, 110–12, 115–16, 123; meditation based on, 50, 87, 89–90, 110–12, 117
Minnesota Study of Twins Raised Apart (MISTRA), 129–30
mistakes, 78, 100, 102, 104, 105, 110, 113, 119; as learning experiences, 103; mea culpa response, 40–41; responsibility for, 21; self-compassion for, 91–92
Mitamura, Takashi, 18–19
moral elevation, 94–95
Mother Teresa, 83
Muir, John, 75

INDEX

NAACP (National Association for the Advancement of Colored People), 15
National Public Radio, 120
nature-nurture overlap, 77, 104, 110, 130
needs: basic, 57, 75, 125; expression of, 23
Neff, Kristen, *Self-Compassion*, 91–92
negative emotions, 4, 5, 6, 10, 127; benefits of, 114, 127; causes and triggers, 57–58, 77–78, 85, 96, 98, 102, 137; expression, 23. *See also specific emotions*
negative emotions management tools: acceptance of emotions, 99, 115–18; acceptance of life, 6, 99, 137; jumping in, 57–60; medication, 128; mental health treatment, 128
negative judgments: body judgments, 92–93, 113; about emotions, 116, 118; needed, 101; as negative emotions cause, 102, 137; negativity bias toward, 99–100
negative judgments, acceptance-based management tools, 4, 6, 96, 99–100, 116, 118, 137; acceptance-promoting core beliefs, 102, 109–10; "big ideas" perspectives, 102–6, 123; disputing exaggerated negative thinking, 102, 106–9, 117, 123; nonjudgmental awareness / mindfulness, 102, 110–12, 123
negotiation, as conflict-resolution tool, 44–45
neuroticism, 130
Newton, Isaac, 72
Nightingale, Florence, 72

no-thanks tool, 23, 26–28, 33, 54
no-way tool, 41–42

older adults: acceptance of life, 99; subjective well-being, 132
online safety, 9
openness personality trait, 130
opinions, expression of, 21, 24, 55; fear of, 18
optimism, 92–93, 94, 98, 107, 135, 137
Oxford Handbook of Happiness, 124
Oxford, University of, 12

panic attacks, 115–16, 118
parents: assertive style, 25–26; bargaining style, 26; of LGBTQ+ children, 86–87; values of, 67, 68, 70, 73
Parkinson's disease, 97–98
Parks, Rosa, 15–16, 18
passivity, 20, 60–61
Peace Corps, 8
persistence, 29–32, 33, 54
personal assertive rights, 21–23, 32–33
personality traits, 130–31
perspective taking, 6, 44, 98, 100; "big idea" tool, 102–6, 123; objective adult approach, 54; as rational compassion, 81–82, 84; for self-acceptance, 91–92, 114; third-party observer approach, 116
pessimism, 131
philanthropy, 82–83
physical activity, mental health benefits, 56
politeness, 18, 19–20, 27–28, 33; pragmatic, 19

positive emotions, 3, 5, 6, 56, 57, 136, 137; benefits, 114, 127–28, 137; expression, 23; as happiness / subjective well-being component, 124, 125, 127–28, 131, 137; information sources about, 124; life circumstances–based, 131; lifespan trends, 132; net sum of, 127; research in, 125, 127–28. *See also specific emotions*
positive psychology, 126
post-traumatic stress disorder (PTSD), 53
prayer, 90, 98, 121
problem-solving skills, 9, 13, 14, 21, 43, 136
professional mental health therapy, 53, 117, 128, 131, 135; for anxiety, 53; for depression, 53, 60, 98, 118–19; imagery rescripting technique, 53–54; self-help *vs.*, 53; for suicidal intentions, 118–19. *See also* cognitive behavioral techniques/therapy (CBT)
prosocial behavior, 79
psychological wealth, 75–76, 125–28
Psychology Today, 120–21

questions: closed-ended, 47–48; demeaning or rude, 33, 34, 36, 37; investigative, 47–48, 55; open-ended, 47, 48, 55; simple, 28–29, 33, 35, 47, 54

racism, 15–16
randomized controlled trials, 6
rejection, as manipulation, 32
religious beliefs/practices, 69, 86–87, 90, 113, 121, 132
respect, 3–4, 6, 9, 13, 21, 34, 49–50, 136; in functional assertiveness, 19–20, 27–28; in self-expression, 52
rest, passive *vs.* active, 60–61
ridicule, 13–14, 17, 32, 33, 34, 36–37
role-playing, 81–82
Roosevelt, Eleanor, 96
rudeness management tools, 32–40; *I*-statements, 33, 34, 35; *maybe*-phrasing, 36, 39, 54; shrugging (verbal or nonverbal), 33–34, 54; simple questions, 33, 35; *you*-statements, 36–38, 39, 54

Salter, Andrew, 24
sarcasm, 33
schedules, 63–66, 76
self, relation to emotions, 116, 117
self-acceptance, 49, 91–92, 99, 113–14
self-attachment, 78
self-care, boundary setting in, 27
self-compassion, 91–93, 113
self-deflation, 133
self-determination, 3–4, 13, 21, 93–94, 136
self-disclosure: for anger control, 45–46; for dealing with shyness, 48–49, 55; honesty in, 27, 48–49; in relationship building, 48–49, 55; through *I*-statements, 24–26; through simple questions, 28–29
self-esteem, 6, 14, 17
self-expression, 52
self-help, *vs.* professional assistance, 53
self-image, 49, 53
self-interest, 26, 78
self-protection, 14
self-reflection, 71
self-respect, 13, 14

self-talk, 115
Seligman, Martin, 126; *Learned Optimism*, 107
sensations, physical: during meditation, 90, 117; mental processing, 125; relation to emotions, 59–60, 99, 115, 116, 118, 125
sharing, 24, 48, 50, 55, 79
shrugging, verbal or nonverbal, 33–34, 54
shyness, 24; definition, 46; *vs.* social anxiety, 50–52
shyness management tools, 24, 32, 131; investigative questions, 47–48, 55; kind communication, 49–50, 55; self-disclosure, 48–49, 55; speaking up, 46–50
Siegel, Ronald, *The Mindfulness Solution*, 117
silence: as acknowledgment of guilt, 41; as manipulation, 32
Smith, Carol, 120–21
Smith, Manuel, 36; *When I Say No, I Feel Guilty*, 8, 21–22
sociability, 46
social anxiety, 4; cultural factors in, 52; *vs.* shyness, 50–52
social anxiety management tools, 14, 50, 51–52; CBT therapy, 11–12, 52; imagery rescripting, 53
social assertiveness. *See* speaking up
social comparison, 133–34
social media posts, 39–40
social well-being, 1, 13, 124
social world, 1, 3, 10
Socrates, 18, 45
speaking up (social assertiveness), 1, 3–4, 5, 8–9, 12, 105; benefits, 13–14, 136; definition, 4, 6, 13; effect on emotions, 6;
as human right, 23; with kindness, 86; trauma and, 52–54
speaking-up tools: for conflict resolution, 43–46, 55; core tools, 23–32, 54; for criticism responses, 32, 40–42, 55; for dealing with shyness, 46–50, 55; *I*-statements, 23–26, 27, 33, 34, 35, 54; for manipulation and rudeness responses, 32–40, 54; no-thanks tool, 23, 26–28, 33, 54; persistence tool, 29–32; simple questions, 28–29, 33, 35, 47, 54; for suicidal intentions, 119
Stewart, Jon, 72
Stoics, 104
subjective well-being. *See* happiness / subjective well-being
suffering, 4, 77–78, 128; children's response to, 79. *See also* compassion (emotional assertiveness); grief
suicide / suicidal thoughts, 9, 87, 118–19
sympathy, 6, 47, 50, 80, 84–85, 89, 91

"this just doesn't matter" perspective, 105–6, 123
thoughts/thinking: as compassion component, 80; evidence-based, 107, 109; exaggerated negative, 102, 106–9, 117, 123; "I can't" thinking, 63, 76, 108; mindfulness in, 92; pessimistic, 131; relation to behavior and emotions, 56, 102
threats, 17–18, 39–40, 77–78
tragedy, personal, 100, 118, 119–22
trauma: as depression trigger, 130; as obstacle to assertive communication, 52–54

UNICEF, 100–101
University of Minnesota, 129–30
University of North Carolina, 115
Ury, William, 44–45

values, 116; disconnection from, 82; domains, 66–67, 68–69, 70, 134; as happiness / subjective well-being component, 125; inherited, 71–72; living up to, 66–76, 82–83; pockets of time and, 73–76; values and goals notebook, 71
verbal assertiveness. *See* speaking up

White supremacy, 15–16
Wilson, Kelly, 67
women: assertive behavior, 16–17; women's rights movement, 16–17; young, human rights of, 23
World Health Organization, 11
worry, 46, 51, 57, 75, 77, 78, 102, 106, 112, 115, 137

Yoshinaga, Naoki, 10–12, 86, 107–8; social anxiety treatment research, 11–12, 52
young people: social assertiveness skills, 9–10; social media–related anxiety, 40; suicide among, 9, 87
Yousafzai, Malala, 23
you-statements, 36–38

Zen, Soto school of, 85
Zenjo, Dōgen, 85
Zeno, 104